THE MR. FOOD®
COOKBOOK

The

MR. FOOD®

C O O K B O O K

Art Ginsburg
—MR. FOOD®

WILLIAM MORROW AND COMPANY, INC.
New York

Library of Congress Cataloging-in-Publication Data

Ginsburg, Art.
  The Mr. Food® cookbook / Art Ginsburg.
    p.   cm.
  ISBN 0-688-09258-6
  1. Cookery.   2. Mr. Food.   I. Title.
TX714.G56   1990
641.5—dc20   90-37528
                                                          CIP

Printed in the United States of America

17 18 19 20

BOOK DESIGN BY RICHARD ORIOLO

To My Family

They Started Me,
They're Sustaining Me,
They're Preserving Me.

Acknowledgments

My special thanks to those who have shared some of their goodies with me and who have graciously allowed me to share them with you. Thanks also to the wonderful public relations people who do such a great job of keeping me informed of the super products available. They all make my time in the kitchen so much easier and more fun:

Epcot Center's Mexican Pavilion at Walt Disney World

Epcot Center's United Kingdom Pavilion at Walt Disney World

The R. T. French Company

McCormick and Co., Inc.

Italian Rose Garlic Products, Inc.

Pepperidge Farm, Inc.

Beatrice Cheese, Inc. (makers of County Line Cheese)

Naturally Yours Yogurt

Western Research Kitchens

Richardson Foods Corporation (makers of Mrs. Richardson's Toppings)

Jarlsberg Cheese

Dole

Bertolli Olive Oil

Keebler Company

Borden, Inc.

J. R. Brooks & Son, Inc.

The California Pistachio Commission

The North Carolina Department of Agriculture

The American Spice Trade Association

The American Dairy Association and
Dairy Council

The Florida Seafood Council

The Texas Department of Agriculture

The California Honey Advisory Board

The California Turkey Industry Board

The Kansas Beef Council

The Gilroy Garlic Festival

The Florida Department of Agriculture

CPC International

Special thanks to those people who were kind enough to share their family recipes with me.

And to Carol and Caryl, 'cause without their organization and patience, I'd still be on the first page.

Contents

Introduction

Usually when we buy a cookbook we're lucky if we can get one or maybe two recipes from it that become our standards. Well, this one will be different. You'll keep this one right at your fingertips and use it over and over again—not for just one or two recipes but for anytime and every time you ask yourself the continual kitchen questions, "What should I make?" "What can I make in a hurry?" "What'll I make for a go-along?" "What can I make that's gourmet looking or tasting but not gourmet difficult?" "How can I get Momma's old-time tastes in a quick throw-together?" Okay, you've got it . . .

BECAUSE

there are a lot of easy recipes and cooking ideas in here, all of them the most popularly requested ones from the past few years of my syndicated TV show, *MR. FOOD.*®

Today, with all the foods and appliances we've got, cooking doesn't have to be difficult. Sure, Grandma started everything from scratch—but she had to, we don't. Once in a while that's nice, though—as long as we keep it easy. With our busy lives today we can still make things taste just the way we like them, without the time and mess.

Healthy cooking is easier than ever, too. Meat is raised, processed, and trimmed to be leaner today, so that means less fat and less cholesterol. An abundance of fresh fruit and vegetables is available to us all year long (and when something we want isn't available fresh, it's a good bet that there's a good-quality supply of it frozen). We're getting produce from all around the world brought to us within days, because of super new growing and transportation methods. We've got the most rigorous food inspection systems ever. And we've got research going on that'll give us a lot of "more" and "better" in the future. Why, even canned goods are undergoing new packing processes that keep them crunchy-fresh and low in salt. It all means more good and tasty food for us!

Almost all of the recipes here can be easily adapted to use what you can and can't eat. For instance, the people watching their cholesterol can usually substitute skim milk for the listed milk or cream, and boneless, skinless chicken breasts can almost always be used when the recipe simply calls for "chicken breasts." Not supposed to have too much salt? Either cut it down or eliminate it from the recipe altogether. It's up to you. Just let your plain old common sense tell you. It's the basic recipe idea that's so important—after that, do your own thing.

Today we're learning all about foods from around the country and around the world. Today we can enjoy the different flavors of every region of the world—and not only in a nearby restaurant but in our own kitchens. The markets have everything on their shelves from Danish cheeses to Japanese noodles, from seasonings for Tex-Mex barbecue to New England clam chowder—no boring dishes that way!

What it all comes down to is if we're sensible, we can excitingly eat

> better than ever before,
> healthier than ever before,
> easier than ever before.

And will this book ever help! We'll be heroes in our own kitchens. How and what we cook and serve and how we simply garnish can make our meals exciting, and we don't have to spend all our time in the kitchen, just a little smart time.

Someone once said that the secret to good food is loving the food you're making or the person you're making it for. Wasn't that Momma's secret? So, have fun in the kitchen and you'll always say **OOH it's so GOOD!!**™

Taste of Adventure

Getting tired of the same old thing? No need to—any dish can be varied and made even better by using the most important tool in our kitchens: the spice rack. Spices and herbs add a taste of adventure to whatever we make, and they are often the difference between boring and exciting.

Here's a chart that can help you on your spice and herb adventure. Have fun with it and enjoy all the **OOH it's so GOOD!!**™

TIDBIT: When using herbs, remember that dried herbs are twice as powerful as fresh herbs. So, for example, if a recipe calls for 2 tablespoons of fresh chopped basil, we could use 1 tablespoon of dried basil instead. And, if a recipe calls for 1 tablespoon of a dried herb, we'll need 2 tablespoons of the fresh herb.

"Flavorprints"
The spices and herbs that distinguish national cuisines*

ITALIAN
Garlic
Basil
Oregano
Parsley
Rosemary
Bay Leaves
Nutmeg
Fennel Seed
Red Pepper
Marjoram
Sage

MEXICAN
Chilies
Oregano
Cumin Seed
Sesame Seed
Cinnamon
Coriander Leaves
   (Cilantro)

RUSSIAN
Dillweed
Coriander Leaves
   (Cilantro)
Parsley
Mint

CHINESE
Ginger
Anise Seed
Garlic
Red Pepper
Sesame Seed
Star Anise

FRENCH
Tarragon

* Based on spices and herbs commonly available in the United States.
Note: All cuisines use black pepper and onion.

Chervil
Parsley
Thyme
Rosemary
Nutmeg
Saffron
Bay Leaves
Garlic
Green and Pink
  Peppercorns

GERMAN
Caraway Seed
Dillweed and Seed
Cinnamon
Ginger
Nutmeg
White Pepper
Juniper Berries
Allspice
Mustard Seed
  and Powder

MIDDLE EASTERN
Allspice
Oregano
Marjoram
Mint
Sesame Seed
Garlic
Dillweed
Cinnamon
Cumin Seed
Coriander Seed
  and Leaves
  (Cilantro)
Anise Seed

SPANISH
Saffron
Paprika
Garlic
Parsley
Cumin Seed

SCANDINAVIAN
Cardamom Seed
Nutmeg
Dillweed and Seed
White Pepper
Mustard Seed

NORTH AFRICAN
Red Pepper
Cumin Seed
Coriander Seed
  and Leaves
  (Cilantro)
Mint
Saffron
Garlic
Cinnamon
Ginger
Turmeric

HUNGARIAN
Paprika
Poppy Seed
Caraway Seed
Garlic
White Pepper

INDIAN
Red Pepper
Chilies
Saffron

Mint
Cumin Seed
Coriander Seed
  and Leaves
  (Cilantro)
Garlic
Turmeric
Curry Powder
Nutmeg
Cinnamon
Ginger
Anise Seed
Dillweed
Cloves
Mace
Cardamom Seed
Mustard Seed
Sesame Seed
Fenugreek

INDONESIAN
Chilies
Garlic
Red Pepper
Bay Leaves
Ginger
Coriander Seed
Turmeric
Curry Powder

GREEK
Oregano
Mint
Garlic
Cinnamon
Dillweed
Nutmeg

Courtesy of the American Spice Trade Association

APPETIZERS

Ah, the appetizers! How many times have we heard, "Gee, I could just eat the appetizers and forget the meal"? Well, in some cases, like cocktail parties or light patio parties, that's great. In most cases, though, appetizers are the tantalizers, the warm-ups, the priming for the big stuff to come. Either way, they set the tone for how you entertain—homey, fancy, whatever. And they don't have to be expensive and gourmet-difficult. Simple, friendly-looking, and ample can convey more than a French chef–made appetizer. A real tasty meatball that tastes like Momma's will win a lot more friends than caviar. That proves that it can be something simple, too. All the appetizers in this chapter are guaranteed easy ones to prepare. If some happen to be fancy-looking—ha! ha!—they're still easy!

Light Apricot Wings

6 to 8 servings

Here's an easy party hors d'oeuvre—crispy, glazed, and right-up-to-the-minute—well, you know how popular wings are!

3 **pounds chicken wings (about 12 to 15)**

APRICOT SAUCE

1 **can (17 ounces) apricot halves, drained**

2 **tablespoons ketchup**

2 **tablespoons vegetable oil**

1 **tablespoon lemon juice**

1 **teaspoon salt**

½ **teaspoon liquid smoke (optional)**

½ **teaspoon hot pepper sauce (optional)**

Preheat oven to 425°F. Split the wings at each joint and discard tips; rinse, then pat dry. Combine all the sauce ingredients in a blender or food processor; blend until smooth. Place chicken wings in a single layer on a rack in a shallow baking pan; brush with Apricot Sauce. Bake for about 30 minutes until brown and crisp, basting with sauce after 15 minutes.

NOTE: I like to put these wings under the broiler for a couple of minutes to give them a nice, crispy glaze. Liquid smoke is usually found in supermarket condiment sections.

Chicken Wings Buffalo-Style

about 5 to 6 servings

Bake or fry: Whichever you decide, it's the easiest, no-mess, sure-fire batch of fun you could serve to anybody.

2½ pounds chicken wings (about 10 to 12)

4 tablespoons (2 ounces) hot pepper sauce (for hotter wings, use up to ¾ cup [6 ounces])

4 tablespoons (¼ cup) butter or margarine, melted

Vegetable oil (for deep-fry method only)

No-Fry Method:

Preheat oven to 325°F. Split the wings at each joint and discard tips; rinse, then pat dry. Place in a single layer in a shallow baking pan. Bake wings, uncovered, for 30 minutes. Remove from pan and place in a large bowl. In a small bowl, combine the hot pepper sauce and melted butter; pour over wings. Cover and marinate in the refrigerator for at least 3 hours or overnight, turning several times. Preheat broiler. Remove wings from marinade, reserving marinade. Place wings on a sheet pan and broil for about 5 minutes on each side, brushing occasionally with marinade, until brown and crisp. Brush with remaining marinade before serving.

Deep-Fry Method (Original Buffalo-Style):

Split the wings at each joint and discard tips; rinse, then pat dry. Deep fry at 400°F for 12 minutes or until cooked through and crispy. Place on paper towels to drain. In a small bowl, combine the hot pepper sauce and melted butter. Toss wings in sauce to coat completely.

NOTE: Don't have a thermometer? Maybe you do—an electric skillet or wok gives you a controlled temperature.

Glazed Chicken Wings

10 to 12 servings

Chicken wings have become a quick-fix favorite. This is one way your family is sure to love them—and it's so easy! Chicken wings again? Why not? Everybody's glad to see them and they always thank you for them.

5 pounds chicken
  wings (20 to 25),
  thawed if frozen

SAUCE
  2 cups mild barbecue
  sauce

½ cup teriyaki sauce

½ teaspoon ground
  ginger

¼ cup honey

Preheat broiler. Split the wings at each joint and discard tips; rinse, then pat dry. Combine all sauce ingredients and set aside. Arrange wings in a single layer in shallow baking pans. Reserve about half the sauce, and brush wings generously with remaining sauce. Broil wings 4 to 5 minutes per side, or until crisp. Serve with reserved sauce for dipping.

Garlicky Chicken Wings

4 to 5 servings

If you like garlic as much as I do, this is just for you. If you like wings, like me, this is just for you. Wings and garlic—can't miss!

- 2 pounds chicken wings (about 8 to 10)
- 3 bulbs fresh garlic, separated into cloves and peeled
- 1 cup plus 1 tablespoon olive oil
- 1 teaspoon salt
- ¼ teaspoon hot pepper sauce
- 1 cup grated Parmesan cheese
- 1 cup seasoned bread crumbs
- 1 teaspoon pepper

Preheat oven to 375°F. Split the wings at each joint and discard tips; rinse, then pat dry. Place the garlic, 1 cup olive oil, salt, and hot pepper sauce in a blender or food processor and purée. Pour into a bowl. In a separate bowl, mix together the Parmesan cheese, bread crumbs, and pepper. Grease a shallow nonstick baking pan with the remaining 1 tablespoon olive oil. Dip the wings, one at a time, in the garlic purée, then roll them in the bread crumb mixture, coating them thoroughly. Place in baking pan in a single layer. Bake for 50 to 60 minutes until brown and crisp.

NOTE: For a quick way to peel garlic, try quick-blanching the cloves in boiling water. The skins should then slip off easily.

First-prize winner in the Annual Gilroy Garlic Festival Recipe Contest

Pepperoni Dip

about 3 cups

Want a fast dip that will have everybody raving? It's done with pepperoni. Know how much everybody loves it on pizza? Well, serve it this way, hot or cold, and they'll call you the master dip maker.

1 can (2.8 ounces) fried onions

2 packages (8 ounces each) cream cheese, softened

1 cup (8 ounces) sour cream

1 package (3½ to 4 ounces) sliced pepperoni, diced

¼ cup minced green bell pepper

¼ teaspoon garlic powder

Preheat oven to 350°F. Reserve ¼ cup fried onions. Mix remaining onions and all other ingredients together. Spread mixture in a 1½-quart casserole dish coated with nonstick vegetable spray. Bake for 20 minutes until heated through. Top with reserved onions.

Baked Party Dip

8 to 12 servings

Your party will be the best one of the year when you serve this special dip baked inside a loaf of bread. It will be the centerpiece of the table and the centerpiece of the party, too.

1 large round loaf dark bread (about 2 pounds), unsliced

1 bunch scallions, chopped

6 garlic cloves, finely minced

2 tablespoons butter or margarine

1 package (8 ounces) cream cheese, cut into small chunks and softened

2 cups (16 ounces) sour cream

3 cups (12 ounces) grated mild or medium Cheddar cheese

1 can (14 ounces) artichoke hearts (water packed, not marinated), drained and cut into quarters

Garlic bread for serving

Preheat oven to 350°F. Cut a hole about 5 inches in diameter in the top of the bread. (If you wish, make a decorative zigzag pattern.) Reserve crusty part to make top for loaf. Scoop out most of the soft inside portion of the loaf and save for another purpose, such as stuffing or bread crumbs. In a skillet, sauté the scallions and garlic in the butter until scallions wilt. Do not burn! Place the cream cheese in a medium-sized bowl; add the scallions, garlic, sour cream, and Cheddar cheese. Mix well. Fold in the

This was a finalist in the Annual Gilroy Garlic Festival Recipe Contest.

artichoke hearts. Fill hollowed-out bread with this mixture. Replace top of bread and wrap in a double thickness of heavy-duty aluminum foil. Bake for about 1½ to 1¾ hours. Remove foil and top of bread and serve, using thin slices of warm garlic bread as dippers.

NOTE: The best part of this dish is when the dip is gone and all you have left is the bread, which is soaked in all those delicious ingredients. Just break the bread up and pass it around!

House Shrimp Dip

about 3 cups

A perfect all-time pleaser—as succulent and rich as anything from a fine restaurant but even better tasting 'cause you made it your very own self. Serve with your favorite crackers.

1½ pounds cooked shrimp, peeled and deveined	1 tablespoon Worcestershire sauce
2 containers (8 ounces each) whipped cream cheese	2 teaspoons hot pepper sauce
1 cup mayonnaise	2 tablespoons chopped scallion tops

Coarsely chop the shrimp. In a small bowl, combine shrimp and all remaining ingredients. Refrigerate several hours or overnight before serving.

ruit Dip

about 2 cups

We're always looking for something to spark up our fruit salad. Well, here's a fantastic treat for everyone—and any kind of fruit goes with it. And does it ever go. . . .

1 **package (8 ounces) cream cheese, softened**	**Your favorite flavor liqueur to taste (about 1 tablespoon)**
1 **jar (7½ ounces) marshmallow cream**	

In a bowl, mix all the ingredients until smooth and creamy. Refrigerate several hours or until chilled.

NOTE: This dip is especially good with strawberries, but I have also served it with melon balls (cantaloupe and honeydew), grapes, apples, bananas, and mandarin oranges. It's great for fast holiday entertaining!

Pistachio-Smoked Salmon Spread

about 1⅓ cups

This is very rich in old-fashioned flavor but with a touch of today's lightness and freshness. Serve it with croissants, bagels, or pitas and they'll be begging you for the "secret ingredient."

1 **package (8 ounces) cream cheese, softened**

¼ **pound smoked salmon, flaked or finely chopped**

About ½ cup (2½ ounces) pistachios, shelled and chopped (you should have ¼ cup after chopping)

3 **teaspoons lemon juice**

In a bowl, beat the cream cheese with an electric mixer until fluffy. Add all remaining ingredients and mix well. Serve immediately or chill until ready to serve.

Hot Artichoke Spread

about 1 quart

You're ready to invite the gang over for a last-minute party any time as long as you can pull this favorite from the freezer and pop it in the oven. Watch them go crazy! (Warning: habit-forming!)

1 cup mayonnaise

2 cans (14 ounces each) artichoke hearts (water packed, not marinated), drained, or 2 packages (9 ounces each) frozen artichoke hearts, thawed

1 drop hot pepper sauce

1 small garlic clove, minced

1 teaspoon lemon juice

1 cup grated Parmesan cheese

Preheat oven to 350°F. Place all the ingredients in a food processor and blend until smooth. (If using a blender instead of a food processor, stop the machine frequently and scrape down the sides of the container with a rubber spatula. First be sure the blades have stopped completely. Blend just until mixture is smooth.) Coat a 1½-quart baking dish with a nonstick vegetable spray and pour in mixture. Bake for 30 minutes, until lightly browned. Serve on party rye bread.

NOTE: You can also bake this spread in several small baking dishes. After they cool, cover each one with plastic wrap and freeze them for later use. When ready to use, thaw, then remove plastic wrap, and rewarm in the oven or microwave.

California Pistachio-Stuffed Mushrooms

20 mushrooms

They're crunchy, fresh, and fancy—the mushrooms everyone will talk about 'cause they're elegant for sure. Well, the pistachios make sure of that. Ha! Ha! If your guests only knew how easy these are. . . .

20 medium-sized fresh mushrooms

3 tablespoons minced onion

7 tablespoons butter or margarine

⅓ cup dry bread crumbs

About ½ cup (2½ ounces) pistachios, shelled and finely chopped (you should have ¼ cup after chopping)

2 tablespoons chopped fresh parsley

¼ teaspoon dried marjoram, crushed

¼ teaspoon salt

Preheat oven to 350°F. Remove stems from mushroom caps; finely chop stems. In a skillet, sauté stems and the onion in 4 tablespoons butter until tender. Add all remaining ingredients except the remaining butter and mix well. Spoon stuffing into mushroom caps. Place on an ungreased baking sheet. Melt the remaining 3 tablespoons butter and drizzle over mushrooms. Bake for 5 minutes or until hot.

Mexican Buffet

6 to 10 servings as a dip
(depends on how hungry your eaters are!)

Just about everybody's into Tex-Mex and this easy-as-a-snap casserole has to be the perfect blend 'cause everyone—the Do-Like-Tex-Mexers and the Don't-Like-Tex-Mexers—loves it. Made ahead, rewarmed, and served with tortilla chips, it's all the Mexican anyone could hope for. This is a contest winner and you'll see why. So what if it's simple!

1 cup (4 ounces) shredded mild or sharp Cheddar cheese

1 cup (4 ounces) shredded Monterey Jack cheese

1 cup (8 ounces) sour cream

3 ounces cream cheese, softened

1 can (16 ounces) refried beans

½ cup picante sauce (any strength)

2 teaspoons chili powder

½ teaspoon ground cumin

Preheat oven to 350°F. In a small bowl, mix the shredded cheeses together. In a large bowl, combine the sour cream, cream cheese, refried beans, picante sauce, chili powder, and cumin. Mix thoroughly by hand or electric mixer. (Or put all ingredients, except shredded cheeses, in a food processor and blend.) Spread half the bean mixture in an 8-inch square baking dish coated with nonstick vegetable spray. Cover with half the shredded cheese. Add remaining bean mixture; top with remaining cheese. Bake for 20 minutes or until heated through.

NOTE: If you prefer, you can use a little less cumin and chili powder. Sometimes I serve chopped tomatoes and guacamole on the side, and I always serve this dish with tortilla chips.

Queso Fundido

4 servings

What's better than cheese melted over your favorite sausage? Well, with this one it's like being south of the border without ever leaving your kitchen.

¼ pound chorizo sausage (or any kielbasa-type sausage), casings removed

½ pound muenster cheese, cut into thin strips

6 flour tortillas

Preheat broiler. Crumble sausage meat into a heavy skillet and fry, stirring, until it crumbles into small pieces. Drain off fat. In a greased 9-inch glass pie plate, arrange half the cheese strips. Cover with chorizo and top with remaining cheese strips. Place under broiler and broil until cheese is melted. Meanwhile, cut tortillas into quarters and heat as directed on the package. Use pieces of tortilla to scoop up melted cheese and chorizo.

Glazed Meatballs

about 65 meatballs

Toothpicks and cocktail napkins turn these into an instant party. And don't just save them for company, 'cause the family will love them just as much as guests do.

3 slices white bread	SAUCE
⅔ cup milk	½ cup ketchup
2 eggs, slightly beaten	¼ cup maple-flavored syrup
1 tablespoon prepared horseradish	¼ cup soy sauce
1 teaspoon salt	1 teaspoon ground allspice
¼ teaspoon pepper	½ teaspoon dry mustard
1½ pounds ground beef	¼ cup water

Preheat oven to 450°F. In a large bowl, soak the bread in the milk until soft. Stir in the eggs, horseradish, salt, and pepper. Add the beef; mix well. Shape mixture into ¾-inch meatballs. Place on a rack in a shallow baking pan and bake for 10 to 15 minutes. Remove from pan and let cool. In a large saucepan combine sauce ingredients. Stir in meatballs. Heat to boiling, stirring often. Reduce heat; keep warm.

NOTE: For a party, serve in a chafing dish with toothpicks. If you want to make these ahead of time, make sauce and freeze. Arrange cooked meatballs in a single layer on a baking sheet, making sure edges do not touch. Freeze just until firm, then remove from baking sheet, wrap in plastic wrap, and keep frozen until ready to heat in sauce. Thaw frozen sauce before heating.

Mini-Pizza Squares

15 to 20 hors d'oeuvre servings

These are equally great as party hors d'oeuvres or a Saturday lunch for the family—simple, simple, simple but sooo luscious!

- 1 pound ground beef
- 1 pound hot Italian sausage
- 1 pound processed cheese spread (such as Velveeta®)
- ½ teaspoon dried oregano
- ½ teaspoon garlic powder
- ½ tablespoon Worcestershire sauce
- 2 loaves party rye bread

Preheat broiler. In a skillet, brown the beef and sausage over medium-high heat. Drain off grease. Add the cheese and stir until melted. Add the oregano, garlic powder, and Worcestershire sauce; mix well. Lay out the rye bread slices on ungreased baking sheets and distribute mixture evenly over bread slices. Place under broiler until brown.

NOTE: These may be frozen until ready to heat and eat (no thawing necessary; just broil and serve). If you're serving these to a smaller gang, you can easily reduce these quantities.

Stacked Cheese Enchilada

6 servings

Here's a way to have the Tex-Mex taste that's all the rage—fast and easy, too!

SAUCE

1 can (28 ounces) crushed tomatoes

2 tablespoons chili powder

1½ teaspoons ground cumin

10 7-inch flour or corn tortillas

3 cups (12 ounces) shredded Cheddar or Monterey Jack cheese

Preheat oven to 350°F. To make sauce, combine the tomatoes, chili powder, and cumin in a bowl. Spread ¼ cup sauce in the bottom of a 9-inch round baking dish or pie plate; top with 1 tortilla. Spread with about ¼ cup sauce, covering tortilla completely. Sprinkle with about ¼ cup cheese. Repeat with remaining tortillas, sauce, and cheese, ending with cheese. Cover with foil and bake for 20 minutes. Cut into wedges, put on serving plates, and pour any sauce remaining in baking dish over tortilla wedges.

Tortilla Beef Roll-ups

6 servings

This is one of the easiest new Tex-Mex–style appetizers, and it's a sure-fire success at a party. As you can see, it's like a roast beef sandwich with a new coat.

4 12-inch flour tortillas

1 container (8 ounces) bacon-horseradish dip

10 to 12 ounces, roast beef, thinly sliced

Leaf lettuce

Spread 1 side of a tortilla with about 2 tablespoons of the horseradish dip, covering the whole tortilla. Top with 1 or 2 slices of the beef. Spread with another 2 tablespoons dip. Top with lettuce leaves. Roll up the tortilla jelly-roll–style and place seam-side down on a platter. Repeat with remaining tortillas. Cover and refrigerate. Before serving, cut each roll-up into thirds.

Frikadeller (Danish Meatballs)

**about 36 meatballs
(more if you make them teaspoon-sized)**

This is one of my all-time favorite recipes! It's a delicious main dish or a simple party hors d'oeuvre. The first time I had them just like this was in Denmark and I thought they must have been specially seasoned. Unh-uh! Simple—wait 'til you see.

1 pound ground beef

1 pound ground veal or ground pork

1 tablespoon salt

1 teaspoon pepper

¾ cup all-purpose flour

1 medium onion, grated

2 eggs

1½ cups water

4 tablespoons (¼ cup) butter or margarine, melted, plus butter or margarine for frying

In a bowl, combine all the ingredients except the butter and blend thoroughly. Let stand for 15 minutes, to allow the flour to absorb the water. Shape meatballs using a tablespoon dipped in the melted butter. (You can use a teaspoon to get cocktail-size meatballs for a party.) In a large skillet, heat the butter until very hot. Reduce heat to medium and fry meatballs for about 5 minutes per side, until golden brown.

Reuben Turnovers

10 turnovers

A Reuben sandwich is traditionally a grilled corned beef, Swiss cheese, and sauerkraut combo served with Russian dressing on rye bread. Well, these are an hors d'oeuvre or appetizer version—homemade taste, easy to make, and convenient to serve.

1 package (7½ ounces) refrigerated biscuits (10 biscuits)

Your favorite dip

FILLING

1 cup (about 4 ounces) finely diced Kielbasa or Polish sausage

1 can (8 ounces) sauerkraut, rinsed and well drained

½ cup (2 ounces) shredded Swiss cheese

½ teaspoon caraway seed

Preheat oven to 375°F. Combine the sausage and sauerkraut in a medium-sized skillet; cook over medium-low heat for about 5 minutes, stirring occasionally. Remove from heat and stir in the cheese and caraway seed. Let cool slightly. Separate the biscuits and roll each into a 4½-inch circle. Place about 3 tablespoons filling in the center of each circle. Fold the dough over the filling, making sure the edges meet. Press edges together with the tines of a fork to seal. Place turnovers on an ungreased cookie sheet. Bake for 12 to 14 minutes or until golden brown. Serve with your favorite dip.

RELISHES AND SAUCES

Relishes are that little extra touch of special on a table. They're the "You didn't have to," but you wanted to. That's why they enhance any meal. And that dab or drizzle of sauce can be the high taste of the whole meal. It's what shows us to be "gourmet savvy." Oh, yes! Well, here's some easy "You didn't have to" gourmet savvy that'll taste like "gourmet work all day."

Refrigerator Pickles

about 9 cups

Looking for something to do with all those summer cucumbers? Here's a taste that everyone will love, and it's probably the easiest pickle in the world to make. You'll see—it'll become one of your standards.

7 cups sliced cucumbers (about 5 medium cucumbers)

1 cup sliced onion

1 green bell pepper, finely sliced

2 cups sugar

1 cup white vinegar

1 tablespoon salt

1 teaspoon celery seed

Combine the cucumbers, onion, and green pepper in a large bowl. Add the sugar, vinegar, salt, and celery seed; mix well. Cover and refrigerate for at least 24 hours before serving.

NOTE: Pickles will keep for about 3 months in the refrigerator, covered. For a different taste, add either garlic, fresh or dried dill or oregano, or hot pepper sauce with the celery seed.

Cranberry Relish

I'm warning you—once you try this no-cook cranberry relish, you won't want the canned sauce anymore. This has a fresh, alive taste that the canned can't duplicate, and it's so easy to make.

4 cups cranberries
  (fresh or frozen)
  (1 12-ounce bag is
  3 cups)

1 apple, cored but
  unpeeled

1 small seedless
  orange, unpeeled

1¼ to 1½ cups sugar

Put the cranberries, apple, and orange through a food processor. Add the sugar and mix well. Store chilled until ready to serve.

Fresh Corn Relish

6 to 8 servings

You're gonna think you're on an August picnic all year long—the fresh corn taste will do that.

8 ears fresh corn, husked

½ cup vegetable oil

¼ cup cider vinegar

1½ teaspoons fresh lemon juice

¼ cup chopped fresh parsley

2 teaspoons salt

2 teaspoons sugar

½ teaspoon dried basil

¼ teaspoon cayenne pepper

2 large tomatoes, peeled and coarsely chopped

½ cup chopped green bell pepper

½ cup chopped scallions

Bring a large kettle of water to a boil over high heat. Add the corn, cover, and return to a boil. Remove kettle from heat and let stand for 5 minutes. Drain corn and let cool. In a large bowl, mix the oil, vinegar, lemon juice, parsley, salt, sugar, basil, and cayenne pepper. Cut cooled corn off cob and add to mixture. Add the tomatoes, green pepper, and scallions. Mix well, cover, and chill for several hours. Serve in a bowl lined with salad greens.

Sweet Pepper Sauce

about 1½ cups

Know how all the fancy restaurants are charging a special price for your pasta when they serve it with sweet red pepper sauce? Well, you can make it your own special way by adding a touch of fennel seed or nutmeg, some ground oregano, or more or less of any of the other ingredients. Here's how easy. . . .

2 tablespoons olive oil

1 cup chopped onion

1 rib celery with leaves, coarsely chopped

1 garlic clove, minced

1 cup seeded and coarsely chopped tomatoes

½ teaspoon dried thyme

1 jar (16 ounces) roasted sweet red peppers, drained

¼ teaspoon salt

⅛ teaspoon pepper

In a large skillet, heat the olive oil. Sauté the onions and celery over medium heat until golden and wilted. Add the garlic and cook for 30 seconds more. Add the tomatoes, thyme, and roasted peppers. Season with the salt and pepper. Simmer for 20 to 30 minutes or until thickened. Purée in a food processor or blender until smooth.

NOTE: Serve with pasta, seafood, poultry, or eggs.

Teriyaki Marinade

about 1 cup
(enough for 1½ to 2 pounds of meat,
fish or poultry)

Add a little excitement to your grilling. This marinade gives a great taste to whatever you're cooking.

½ cup soy sauce

¼ cup sherry (dry or medium)

2 tablespoons vegetable oil

2 tablespoons sugar or molasses

½ teaspoon ground ginger or ¾ teaspoon freshly grated ginger

1 to 2 garlic cloves, crushed

In a bowl, mix all ingredients together. Cover and refrigerate until ready to use.

NOTE: This marinade is right for almost anything from turkey, chicken, or veal cutlets to thinly sliced beef steak to fresh halibut, swordfish, or tuna steaks. Just place the cutlets or steaks into the marinade and refrigerate for 30 minutes (longer if you want the marinade flavors to be stronger). (Fish takes less time to marinate than meat or chicken.)

Remember, broil fish for 10 minutes per inch at its thickest part.

Steak Marinade

6 to 8 servings
(enough for 3 to 4 pounds steak)

Been looking for an easy steak marinade? Well, wait 'til you hear the raves for this one.

3 cups dry white wine

¾ cup vegetable oil

2 to 3 teaspoons salt

1 tablespoon pepper

1 teaspoon dried rosemary

Pinch of dried sage

Pinch of dried thyme

2 onions, thinly sliced

4 garlic cloves, mashed

In a medium-sized bowl, mix all the marinade ingredients together. Refrigerate marinade until ready to use.

NOTE: Strip steak, sirloin, porterhouse, and rib eye work well. Just pierce the steak all over with a fork or skewer and place in a baking pan. Pour the marinade over the meat. Cover and let marinate for 6 hours in the refrigerator, turning occasionally. Remove the steak from the bowl, reserving the marinade, and grill it to whatever doneness you prefer. Baste the steak with the marinade a few times during grilling.

The garlic just seems to make this marinade. You can cut it down to 2 cloves or hit it with 6, but it's up to you. (You'll love it, though!)

asy Cheese Sauce

about ½ cup

This sauce has so many uses—you'll be able to use it on anything you want to make richer and heartier and, yes, even fancier.

- **4 slices (¾ ounce each) processed yellow American cheese, cut into quarters**
- **¼ cup milk**

- **⅛ teaspoon dry mustard**
- **⅛ teaspoon ground nutmeg**

In a small saucepan, combine all ingredients and cook over medium heat, stirring, until melted.

NOTE: Serve over steak, vegetables, potatoes, pasta, or rice.

Tangy Seafood Sauce

2 cups

A seafood sauce you can also use as a vegetable dip—impossible? Nope—here it is.

- 1 cup mayonnaise
- ½ cup chili sauce
- ¼ cup dry sherry
- ¼ cup chopped fresh parsley
- 1 tablespoon grated onion
- ½ teaspoon Worcestershire sauce

Combine all ingredients in a small bowl and chill.

NOTE: Great served with any cooked and chilled fish.

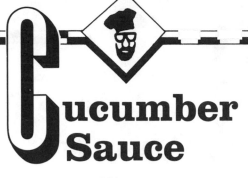

Cucumber Sauce

3½ cups

Good! Another way to use all those cucumbers when they come into season—as fresh as a summer garden, so simple, and so very nice!

2 large cucumbers, peeled, seeded, and grated

2 cups (16 ounces) sour cream

2 teaspoons lemon juice

4 tablespoons chopped fresh dill or 4 teaspoons dried dillweed

1 teaspoon salt, or to taste

¼ teaspoon pepper, or to taste

In a large bowl, combine the cucumbers and sour cream. In a small bowl, mix the lemon juice and dill. Fold into sour cream–cucumber mixture. Season with salt and pepper.

NOTE: Great on poached fish or as a salad dressing.

Quick Fresh Tomato Sauce

enough for 1 pound of pasta

A deliciously fresh-tasting cooked tomato sauce! Try serving it over spaghetti or linguine. This is the kind we find in the fancy Italian restaurants—as easy as it is, we can make it ourselves.

2 garlic cloves, minced

2 celery ribs, thinly sliced

1 red bell pepper, thinly sliced

1 can (2 ounces) anchovies (undrained), chopped

¼ cup olive oil

6 to 8 fresh tomatoes, peeled and diced, or 1 can (28 ounces) crushed tomatoes

1 teaspoon dried basil

¼ teaspoon dried oregano

¼ teaspoon crushed red pepper

2 tablespoons stuffed green olives, coarsely chopped

In a saucepan or large skillet, sauté the garlic, celery, red pepper, and anchovies in the olive oil until just slightly soft. Add the tomatoes, then the basil, oregano, crushed red pepper, and green olives. Cook over low heat for about 20 minutes, or until slightly thickened.

Garlic Pepper Sauce

about 3 cups
(enough for 2 pounds of pasta)

*For all you garlic lovers, here's an easy sauce that's just great with pasta. But make sure your honeybunch enjoys it when you do—then you can love each other . . . you'll have to! Isn't that the true meaning of **OOH** it's so **GOOD!!**™??*

18 garlic cloves, minced

1½ cups olive oil

1 teaspoon crushed red pepper

Salt to taste (optional)

1 can (10¾ ounces) chicken broth

1 teaspoon dried thyme

In a medium-sized saucepan, cook the garlic in the oil for 5 minutes. Stir in pepper and salt. Gradually stir in chicken broth, add thyme, and simmer until heated through. Serve immediately over pasta.

esto Sauce

**about 1½ cups
(enough for 1 pound of pasta)**

Use as a salad dressing, for pasta, or even over boiled potatoes. It's also superb over sliced fresh tomatoes. This is the fancy, sophisticated Italian taste that's so popular now, and it's worth the raves it's getting.

2 cups fresh basil,
  lightly packed

1 cup olive oil

1 cup grated
  Parmesan cheese

2 garlic cloves,
  crushed

1 teaspoon salt

½ cup pine nuts,
  almonds, or
  walnuts, finely
  chopped

Dash of nutmeg
(optional)

Blend all ingredients in blender or food processor until smooth. Store in refrigerator, covered, until ready to use. Mix well before serving; use hot or cold.

SOUPS AND CHOWDERS

Soups and chowders are very "in" right now 'cause veggies, fish, and one-pot suppers are also "in." So are easy cleanup and down-home taste, not to mention hearty and economical meals. And easy preparation is certainly always "in." Reasons enough? Just add a salad and some crisp bread and hear, "Hello, hero!"

TIDBIT: Soups and chowders are ideal for rewarming in the microwave. In fact, they always seem to taste better when they're reheated, so make a large batch and you'll have the second and third meals "ready to go" (and even better than the first time around).

One-Pot French Chowder

6 to 8 servings

Here's a hearty fish chowder—a lot like French bouilla-baisse but much less complicated. Of course, everyone else will think it's so difficult. Well, they'll think it must be—but we'll know better.

¼ cup vegetable oil

1 large onion, chopped

2 garlic cloves, minced

1 cup coarsely chopped celery

¼ cup coarsely chopped fresh parsley

2 cans (29 ounces each) tomato sauce

2 cups dry white wine

2 cans (10¾ ounces each) chicken broth

2 teaspoons dried thyme

1 teaspoon dried sage

¼ teaspoon turmeric (optional)

3 pounds white-fleshed fish fillets (such as cod or haddock), cut into 2-inch chunks

Heat the oil in a Dutch oven. Add the onion, garlic, celery, and parsley, and sauté for about 10 minutes, until softened. Add the tomato sauce, white wine, chicken broth, thyme, sage, and turmeric. Bring to a boil, reduce heat, and simmer for 20 to 25 minutes. Add the fish and simmer for 10 to 15 minutes more.

NOTE: Enjoy with crusty French bread, a green salad, and some cheese and you've got a whole meal.

ouper Stew

6 to 8 servings

Add some cut-up ham, turkey, or roast beef and turn this into a whole-meal stew. It's certainly thick and hearty enough, and it's easy as can be, too.

- 1 **can (28 ounces) crushed tomatoes**
- 1 **tablespoon Italian seasoning**
- ½ **teaspoon onion powder**
- ½ **teaspoon garlic powder**
- ½ **teaspoon salt**
- 1 **bag (16 ounces) frozen mixed vegetables**

- 1 **can (16 ounces) cannellini (white kidney beans), drained**
- 1 **cup cooked tubettini or other small pasta**

  Grated Parmesan cheese for topping (optional)

In a large saucepan, combine the tomatoes, Italian seasoning, onion and garlic powders, and salt; bring to a boil. Reduce heat, cover, and simmer for 10 minutes. Add the vegetables and return mixture to a boil. Reduce heat, cover, and simmer, stirring occasionally, until vegetables are almost tender, about 4 minutes. Stir in beans and pasta. Cover and cook until heated through, about 2 minutes.

NOTE: Put a slice of French or garlic bread in the bottom of each serving bowl and sprinkle some grated Parmesan cheese over the soup if you'd like.

Fisherman's Stew

6 to 8 servings

Try serving this country-style in individual soup bowls over crisp garlic bread—I love it. I even change the taste every few times by using more or less of the various ingredients or by substituting a little oregano or thyme for the bay leaf. Just add a salad and it's a whole meal.

¼ cup olive oil

2 onions, sliced

3 garlic cloves, crushed

1 can (14½ ounces) whole tomatoes

1 can (15 ounces) tomato sauce

1 tablespoon chopped fresh parsley

¼ teaspoon salt

¼ teaspoon pepper

1 teaspoon paprika

1 bay leaf

1½ cups water

½ cup white wine

2½ to 3 pounds white-fleshed fish fillets, such as cod, haddock, sole, or flounder, cut into large chunks (approximately 3 inches each)

Heat the oil in a large saucepan and sauté the onions and garlic until soft. Add the tomatoes, tomato sauce, parsley, salt, pepper, paprika, and bay leaf. Cook, stirring, for 5 to 7 minutes. Add the water, wine, and fish. Bring to a boil and cook for 5 to 6 more minutes, or until fish is cooked through. Remove bay leaf before serving.

Cream of Vegetable Soup

6 to 8 servings

Have extra veggies? Just throw them together and get a presto creamy vegetable soup as rich and fancy-tasting as a "French gourmet" meal.

3½ cups chicken stock

4 cups diced potatoes

1 cup diced celery

1 cup diced carrots

½ cup diced onions or scallions

1 parsnip, diced (optional)

1 tablespoon butter or margarine

1 tablespoon all-purpose flour

Salt and pepper to taste

½ cup heavy cream

Chopped fresh parsley for garnish

In a large pot, combine all ingredients except heavy cream and parsley, and cook until vegetables are tender. Purée batches in a blender or food processor until smooth. Return mixture to the pot and stir in the heavy cream. Heat until piping hot, and serve sprinkled with the parsley.

NOTE: Instead of chicken stock you can use 3½ cups water and a packet of instant soup mix such as chicken, mushroom, leek, or vegetable. Sometimes I like to use 2 cups diced potatoes and 2 cups diced turnips instead of all potatoes. For a flavor change, add a pinch of nutmeg or dried tarragon, rosemary, or thyme with the parsley garnish.

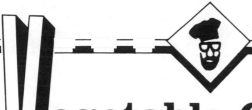

Vegetable Chowder

10 to 12 servings

A no-hassle, easy taste treat for any mealtime. And nobody complains about eating their veggies this way.

3 quarts milk

1 package (10 ounces) frozen chopped broccoli

1 package (10 ounces) frozen corn

1 package (16 ounces) frozen sliced carrots

1 package (10 ounces) frozen peas

1 tablespoon dried basil

1 tablespoon dried marjoram

1 teaspoon white pepper

1 teaspoon onion powder

1 teaspoon salt (optional)

2 cups instant mashed potato buds or flakes

In a large pot, combine all the ingredients except the potato buds or flakes. Bring to a boil, stirring occasionally. Turn heat to low, stir in the potato buds or flakes, and let cook for 3 to 4 more minutes, stirring occasionally. Serve immediately.

NOTE: Add whatever kind or whatever amounts of frozen veggies you'd like. It will work fine. I often add an extra package of broccoli and a package of frozen lima beans along with the others. More seasoning, less seasoning, your favorite seasoning—make it any way at all.

Chicken Soup

8 to 10 servings

One of my most requested recipes—chicken soup just like Momma made (my Momma, anyway).

1 3- to 4-pound chicken, cut up

4 quarts cold water

3 to 4 carrots, cut into chunks

2 to 3 celery ribs, cut into chunks

2 medium-sized onions, cut into chunks

Salt and pepper to taste

Rinse the chicken under cold running water. Put all ingredients in a soup pot and bring to a boil. Lower the heat, cover, and let simmer until chicken meat falls off the bones (about 3 hours).

NOTE: Here are some variations I like:
1. Strain the soup for a clear broth (reserving the chicken meat for another use).
2. Use white pepper instead of black so there are no specks.
3. Use different amounts of any of the vegetables.
4. Add dill or parsley, a couple of parsnips, or garlic cloves—or all of these.
5. Serve the soup with just the veggies in it and use the chicken to make a great salad.

Gazpacho

8 to 10 servings

It's a chilled Spanish salad soup—perfect for the warm weather, and there's nothing to it. It's really as fresh as a summer garden can be.

1 can (46 ounces) tomato juice

1 cup diced cucumber

1 cup diced green bell pepper

1 cup sliced scallions

2 or 3 garlic cloves, finely chopped

6 tablespoons white vinegar

4 tablespoons olive or vegetable oil

2 teaspoons salt

2 teaspoons Worcestershire sauce

Hot pepper sauce to taste

Mix together all ingredients in a large bowl and chill.

NOTE: I like to throw in a chopped fresh tomato. But that's just one of the options, along with any fresh vegetables or your favorite herb, such as thyme, rosemary, oregano, basil, or dill. If you're lucky enough to have fresh basil—chop and add it, too. Wow! Wow! Wow!

Gazpacho Blanco (White Gazpacho)

3 to 4 servings

Looks and sounds fancy but it's just another version of gazpacho—without the tomatoes. Nice novelty, nice conversation piece.

- 2 cucumbers, peeled, seeded, and cut into chunks
- ½ cup chicken broth
- 1 cup (8 ounces) sour cream or plain yogurt
- 4 teaspoons white wine vinegar (or to taste)
- Salt and pepper to taste
- Chopped fresh tomato for garnish
- Chopped scallion for garnish

Purée in batches all ingredients except garnishes in a food processor or blender until smooth. Refrigerate until chilled. Pour into serving bowls and garnish with chopped tomato and scallion.

Vegetable Cheese Chowder

about 6 servings

Here's a simple—but sure to get raves—vegetable chowder that lets you use any combination of veggies. Wanna clean out your refrigerator vegetable bin? Try this.

- 2 **cups water**
- 1 **can (10¾ ounces) chicken broth**
- 1 **cup sliced carrots**
- ½ **cup chopped onion**
- 1 **small garlic clove, minced**
- ⅛ **teaspoon pepper**
- 2 **cups coarsely chopped fresh broccoli**
- 2 **tablespoons all-purpose flour**
- ¾ **cup milk**
- 1½ **cups (6 ounces) shredded Swiss cheese**

Put the water, broth, carrots, onion, garlic, and pepper in a large saucepan. Bring to a boil. Reduce heat, cover, and simmer for 10 minutes. Add the broccoli; return soup to a boil. Meanwhile, combine the flour and milk in a small bowl, stirring well. Slowly add flour mixture to the boiling soup, stirring constantly. Cook over medium heat, stirring occasionally, for 10 minutes, or until thickened and bubbling. Stir in the cheese. Serve immediately.

NOTE: Use any combination of veggies—fresh, frozen, or even leftovers. If using cooked vegetables, add them after stirring the flour mixture into the soup base.

Fish and Rice Chowder

8 to 10 servings

Easy???!!!—Just throw everything into a pot and let it cook. Now, isn't that easy enough?

1¼ cups uncooked long-grain white rice

2½ cups tomato sauce

3¾ cups water

2 cups raw mixed vegetables, cut into chunks

1¼ pounds fish fillets, cut into 1-inch pieces

2 teaspoons salt

¼ teaspoon pepper

1 bay leaf

Mix together all ingredients in a large saucepan or soup kettle; bring to a vigorous boil. Turn heat to low; cover and simmer gently for 15 to 20 minutes, until rice is cooked and vegetables are tender. If a thinner chowder is desired, add additional water. Remove bay leaf before serving.

NOTE: You can use any kind of fish fillets. You might want to try cod, haddock, or perch.

Easy Potato Soup

8 to 10 servings

Delicious, hearty, and easy! Make it your own way—want to add some broccoli, peas, or green beans? Go ahead! (And it tastes even better the second day.)

4 tablespoons (¼ cup) butter or margarine

1½ cups diced onions

4 cups diced potatoes

1 or 2 carrots, coarsely grated

2 cups water

1 teaspoon salt

½ teaspoon pepper

1 teaspoon dried dillweed

3 cups milk

2 tablespoons chopped fresh parsley

Instant potato flakes or buds (optional)

In a large saucepan, melt the butter. Sauté the onions until golden. Add the potatoes, carrots, water, salt, pepper, and dillweed. Bring to a boil, reduce heat to low, and simmer until potatoes are tender, about 25 to 30 minutes (or longer if you want the potatoes creamy). Stir in the milk and parsley and heat until hot. If you want a thicker soup, stir in some instant potato flakes or buds during the last few minutes of cooking.

CHICKEN AND TURKEY

We're eating more and more poultry every year, and we're always looking for more and more ways to make it. Sure, all of our regular favorite recipes are grand, but to keep them our favorites, we have to have some variety, some excitement, and some adventure once in a while. That's how some of those "once in a whiles" become our new favorites.

Chicken and turkey are amazingly versatile, and they're a great health choice besides. Almost every seasoning and cooking method works wonderfully with them, so imagine how many combinations that gives us. We get many different combos, plus easy, plus yummy. Wait 'til you try some of these, especially when they help you out of the jam of "My gosh! What can I make fast?" That's when you get the plus of **OOH it's so GOOD!!**™

TIDBIT: Remember that there's no such thing as medium rare when it comes to poultry. It should be cooked through. Then it'll be better tasting and better for you.

Timetable for
Roasting Chicken at 350°F.

Parts	Approx- imate Weight	Final Meat Thermo- meter Reading (in degrees F.)	Approximate Cooking Time* (in minutes)
Whole (unstuffed)	3½ lbs.	185 to 190	1 hr. 15 min.
(stuffed)	3½ lbs.	185 to 190	1 hr. 40 min.
(cut-up)†	3½ lbs.	180	50 to 60
4 Thighs	4½ to 6½ oz. each	180	45 to 50
4 Thighs (boneless)	3½ to 5½ oz. each	160	30 to 35
4 Breast Halves	8 to 10 oz. each	180	50 to 55
4 Breast Halves (boneless)	5 to 7 oz. each	160	30 to 35
4 Drumsticks	3½ to 5½ oz. each	180	45 to 50
4 Leg-Thigh combinations	8½ to 10½ oz. each	185 to 190	50 to 55
4 Quarters (2 breasts, 2 leg-thighs)	12 to 14 oz. each	185 to 190	60 to 65

* Cooking times are based on chicken taken directly from the refrigerator.
† Approximate weight of pieces of a cut-up 3½-lb. broiler-fryer chicken:

Thighs	5 to 6 oz. each
Drumsticks	3½ to 4 oz. each
Breasts with rib (halves)	9 to 10 oz. each
Wings	3 to 4 oz. each
Whole back	8 to 9 oz. each

Courtesy of the National Broiler Council

Timetable for Roasting
A Whole Turkey

As simple as 1—2—3!

Turkey is one of today's best meat buys, both nutritionally and economically. Whole turkeys are sold oven-ready: dressed, washed, inspected, and packaged. After turkeys leave the processing plant, no hands touch them until time for kitchen preparation.

It takes only 6 minutes to prepare a defrosted whole turkey for roasting (without stuffing).

If stuffing is desired, it's often best prepared separately, placed in a covered casserole, and cooked with the turkey during the last hour of roasting time.

Follow label instructions for roasting, or use these simple directions to obtain a beautiful golden brown, ready-to-carve-and-eat turkey:

1. **Thawing**: (If turkey is not frozen, begin with step 2.) *Do not thaw poultry at room temperature.* Leave turkey in original packaging and use one of the following methods:

No hurry: Place wrapped turkey on tray in refrigerator for 3 to 4 days; allow 5 hours per pound of turkey to completely thaw.

Fastest: Place wrapped turkey in sink and cover with cold water. Allow about ½ hour per pound of turkey to completely thaw. Change water frequently.

Refrigerate or cook turkey when it is thawed. Refreezing uncooked turkey is not recommended.

Commercially frozen stuffed turkeys should *not* be thawed before roasting.

2. **Preparation for roasting**: All equipment and materials used for storage, preparation, and serving of poultry must be clean. Wash hands thoroughly with hot soapy water before and after handling raw poultry. Use hard plastic or acrylic cutting boards to prepare poultry.

Remove plastic wrapping from thawed turkey. Remove giblets and neck from the body and neck cavities. To remove neck, it may be necessary to release legs from band of skin or wire hock lock. Rinse turkey inside and out with cool water, pat dry with a paper towel, and return legs to hock lock or band of skin; or tie together loosely. Tuck tips of wings under back of turkey. Neck skin should be skewered with a poultry pin or round toothpick to back of turkey to provide a nice appearance for serving at table. The turkey is now completely ready for roasting.

3. **Open pan roasting**: Place turkey breast-side up on flat rack in shallow roasting pan, about 2 inches deep. Insert meat thermometer deep into thickest part of thigh next to body, not touching bone.

Brush turkey skin with vegetable oil to prevent drying. Turkey is done when meat thermometer registers 180 to 185°F. and drumstick is soft and moves easily at joint.

Roasting at 325°F.

Approximate Weight (in pounds)	Approximate Cooking Time* (in hours)
6 to 8	2¼ to 3¼
8 to 12	3 to 4
12 to 16	3½ to 4½
16 to 20	4 to 5
20 to 24	4½ to 5½

Once skin of turkey is golden brown, shield breast loosely with rectangular-shaped piece of lightweight foil to prevent overbrowning.

* Approximate Roasting Time: Factors affecting roasting times are type of oven, oven temperature, and degree of thawing. Begin checking turkey for doneness about one hour before end of recommended roasting time.

Courtesy of the California Turkey Industry Board

Chicken Breast Scampi

4 to 6 servings

Yes, scampi. No, No, not shrimp—chicken scampi. Try it over some rice or spaghetti to sop up that garlic sauce.

2 to 3 pounds chicken breasts, boned and skinned

½ pound (2 sticks) butter or margarine

4 garlic cloves, minced

2 scallions, minced

1 tablespoon chopped parsley

2 teaspoons fresh dill *or* 1 teaspoon dried dillweed

½ teaspoon oregano

½ teaspoon salt

½ teaspoon pepper

Preheat oven to 350°F. Cut the chicken breasts into approximately 2"x1" pieces and place in a 9"x13" baking dish. Melt the butter in a saucepan over low heat. Add the garlic, scallions, parsley, dill, oregano, salt, and pepper, and cook for 2 minutes. Pour the mixture over the chicken pieces. Bake for 10 minutes, turn chicken pieces over, and bake for another 10 minutes. Turn oven to broil and put chicken under broiler for 3 to 4 minutes or until lightly browned.

Chicken Breast with Honey-Wine Sauce

4 servings

This sounds, looks, and tastes so fancy that the company will think you worked hard all day—we'll keep it our little secret.

1 cup dry white wine	½ cup all-purpose flour
4 tablespoons soy sauce	1 teaspoon salt
¼ teaspoon garlic powder	½ teaspoon pepper
4 chicken breasts, skinned, boned, and cut into chunks about 2"x1"	4 tablespoons vegetable oil
	½ cup honey

In a large bowl, mix the wine, soy sauce, and garlic powder. Add the chicken pieces, stir to coat, and marinate for 1 hour in the refrigerator. Drain chicken, reserving marinade. In a shallow dish, mix the flour, salt, and pepper. Lightly dredge the chicken, one piece at a time, in the seasoned flour. In a large frying pan, heat the oil until moderately hot. Add the chicken and cook, turning, until brown on all sides. Add the honey to the reserved marinade and pour over chicken. Cover and simmer for about 15 to 20 minutes or until tender. Transfer chicken to serving platter and spoon sauce over.

Chicken Pie

6 servings

Here's down-home, country-style goodness. It will make you look so old-fashioned kitchen-y. If they only knew how easy it was!

3 cups shredded or diced cooked chicken

1¼ cups milk

½ cup (4 ounces) sour cream

1 can (10¾ ounces) condensed cream of chicken soup

¾ cup biscuit baking mix

¼ cup cornmeal

1 egg

2 cups (8 ounces) shredded Cheddar cheese

Paprika (optional)

Preheat oven to 375°F. In a saucepan, combine the chicken, ½ cup of the milk, sour cream, and soup and bring to a boil. Spoon mixture into 6 ungreased 10-ounce casserole dishes or custard cups, or pour into an ungreased 9"x13" baking dish. In a large bowl, beat the remaining ¾ cup milk and the baking mix, cornmeal, and egg until almost smooth. Pour evenly over hot chicken mixture. Sprinkle with the cheese and paprika. Bake, uncovered, for 20 to 25 minutes or until top is set and soup mixture bubbles around edges.

Winner in the Bisquick® Invitational Recipe Contest

Turkey Buffet

4 to 6 servings

Leftover turkey? Here's the easiest way to turn leftovers into something special. Everyone will love it. Try it— you'll see!

3 cups cubed cooked turkey	½ teaspoon salt
1 package (10 ounces) frozen peas, cooked and drained	Dash pepper
	½ cup mayonnaise
1 cup (4 ounces) grated Cheddar cheese	1 large fresh tomato, peeled and cut into 6 slices
¼ cup chopped onion	¾ cup crushed potato chips
1 tablespoon lime juice	

Preheat oven to 350°F. In a large bowl, combine the turkey, peas, ½ cup of the cheese, onion, lime juice, seasonings, and mayonnaise; mix lightly. Spread in an ungreased 6"x10" baking dish and top with tomato slices. Bake for 25 minutes. Combine remaining ½ cup cheese and the potato chips and sprinkle over top of casserole. Bake for 3 to 5 minutes more, or until cheese is melted.

NOTE: Here's an easy way to peel fresh tomatoes: Remove the stems, dip tomatoes in boiling water for about 15 seconds, then plunge them into cold water; the skins will slip off easily. But be careful: Don't burn yourself when removing the tomatoes from the boiling water.

Chicken and Rice Pot

4 to 6 servings

To give this recipe that fresh garden taste, I like to add sliced fresh mushrooms and maybe some fresh basil, rosemary, or dill. It's an easy, make-ahead summer dinner, so there's no fussing at dinnertime.

- 1 can (10¾ ounces) condensed cream of mushroom soup
- 2 cups water
- 1 cup uncooked long-grain white rice
- 2 tablespoons chopped fresh parsley

- 1 3- to 4-pound chicken, cut into 8 pieces
- 1 envelope (1.25 ounces) dried onion soup mix

Preheat oven to 350°F. In a medium-sized bowl, mix the mushroom soup, water, rice, and parsley. Pour into bottom of roaster pan or large casserole dish. Place the chicken pieces on top. Sprinkle the soup mix over chicken. Cover and bake for about 1½ hours or until chicken is done.

Cranberry Chicken Loaf

4 to 6 servings

This looks like an ordinary meat loaf, but it's an all-in-one holiday meal.

½ cup firmly packed brown sugar

½ cup whole-berry cranberry sauce

2 pounds ground chicken or turkey

¾ cup (6 ounces) evaporated milk

2 tablespoons bottled steak sauce

2 tablespoons ketchup

1 teaspoon prepared mustard

¾ cup cracker crumbs

2 eggs

Salt and pepper to taste

½ teaspoon Italian seasoning

½ teaspoon garlic powder (or to taste)

2 tablespoons diced onion

Preheat oven to 350°F. Grease a 9-inch loaf pan. Sprinkle the brown sugar over the bottom of the pan. Spread the cranberry sauce evenly over the sugar; set aside. In a large bowl, combine all the remaining ingredients; mix thoroughly. Shape mixture into loaf and set in pan on top of cranberry sauce. Pat down top of loaf until smooth and firm. Bake for 55 to 60 minutes or until done. Let set in pan for about 5 minutes, then invert loaf onto a serving platter.

NOTE: The sugar and the cranberry sauce combine to make a rich sweet-and-sour topping.

ancy Fast Chicken

6 servings

Last-minute company coming? Fancy Fast Chicken is just the answer! There's crunch, there's richness, there's elegance, and it's so darn easy. I like to add a few sliced mushrooms so it will taste homemade-fresh.

- 3 whole chicken breasts, split and skinned
- 6 slices Swiss cheese (1 ounce each)
- ¼ pound fresh mushrooms, sliced (optional)
- 1 can (10¾ ounces) condensed cream of chicken soup
- ½ cup dry white wine
- 2 cups herbed stuffing mix
- 8 tablespoons (1 stick) butter or margarine, melted

Preheat oven to 350°F. Place the chicken in a lightly greased 9″x13″ baking dish. Top each piece with a slice of Swiss cheese. Arrange the sliced mushrooms over the cheese. Mix the soup and the wine and pour over chicken. Sprinkle the stuffing mix over the top, and drizzle on the melted butter. Bake for 50 to 60 minutes, or until chicken is cooked through.

NOTE: I have found that if I use boneless chicken breasts I have to bake them for only about 45 to 50 minutes.

Chicken Picante

6 servings

You don't have to go out to enjoy Tex-Mex food—just try this easy-as-can-be chicken recipe. It's got that Tex-Mex influence at its best—perfect for that easy something-different-for-a-change meal.

3 whole chicken breasts, split, skinned, and boned

2 tablespoons butter or margarine

6 tablespoons plain yogurt (optional)

1 lime, peeled and sliced into 6 wedges

Chopped cilantro or fresh parsley for garnish

MARINADE

½ cup medium hot chunky taco sauce

¼ cup Dijon mustard

2 tablespoons fresh lime juice

In a large bowl, mix together all the marinade ingredients. Add the chicken, turning to coat. Marinate in refrigerator for at least 30 minutes or up to 1½ hours. In a large skillet, heat butter until foamy. Remove chicken from marinade, reserving marinade, and add to skillet. Cook for about 10 minutes over medium-high heat, turning to brown on all sides. Add marinade to pan and cook about 5 minutes more, until fork can be inserted into chicken with ease and marinade is slightly reduced. Remove chicken to warmed serving platter. Raise heat to high and boil marinade for 1 minute; pour over chicken. Place 1 tablespoon yogurt on each breast half and top each with a lime wedge. Garnish with chopped cilantro or parsley.

National Chicken Cooking Contest Grand Prize Winner

Stuffed Chicken Quarters

4 to 6 servings

It doesn't have to be a big special day when we stuff a chicken. Here's an everyday simple recipe that'll shout "Special!" with every bite.

- 2 medium zucchini, shredded
- 3 tablespoons butter or margarine
- 4 slices white bread, torn into small pieces
- 1 egg, beaten
- 1 cup (4 ounces) shredded Swiss cheese
- 1/8 teaspoon pepper
- 4 to 6 chicken quarters (thighs or breasts)

Preheat oven to 400°F. Sauté the zucchini in the butter in a 2-quart saucepan until tender. Remove from heat and add the bread, egg, cheese, and pepper; mix well. Loosen the skin of each chicken quarter to form a pocket; spoon stuffing mixture into pocket. Put chicken in an ungreased 9"x13" baking pan and bake, uncovered, for 1 hour, or until chicken is cooked through.

Sweet-and-Sour Chicken

4 servings

This works great with almost any veggies or seasonings, and with the short cooking time everything stays summer-crunchy.

1 can (20 ounces) pineapple chunks in natural juice, drained and juice reserved

3 to 4 tablespoons Worcestershire sauce

2 tablespoons ketchup

1 tablespoon cornstarch

1 tablespoon honey

2 tablespoons vegetable oil

2 whole chicken breasts, split, skinned, boned, and cut into 1-inch cubes

1 red or green bell pepper, cut into thin strips

3 scallions, cut into 1-inch pieces

In a medium-sized bowl combine the reserved pineapple juice and the Worcestershire sauce, ketchup, cornstarch, and honey; mix well. Heat the oil in a large skillet. Add the chicken; stir-fry over high heat until lightly browned. Add the pepper; cook 2 minutes. Add the pineapple juice mixture, then the pineapple chunks and scallions. Cook, stirring, for 1 to 2 minutes, or until sauce thickens slightly.

NOTE: Serve over rice.

Lemon Grilled Chicken

4 servings

It's barbecue-satisfying but light and fresh at the same time. What a nice change from the normally heavy barbecue items.

1 3- to 4-pound chicken, quartered

MARINADE
½ cup lemon juice
5 teaspoons sugar
1 teaspoon olive oil
1 bay leaf

½ teaspoon salt
½ teaspoon poultry seasoning
½ teaspoon dried basil
¼ teaspoon pepper

In a small saucepan, mix together all the marinade ingredients; cook, stirring constantly, over medium heat for 2 to 3 minutes. Let cool to room temperature. Place chicken quarters in a single layer in a large shallow dish. Pour marinade over chicken. Cover and marinate in refrigerator for 1 to 2 hours. Remove chicken from marinade, reserving marinade, and place skin-side up on a preheated barbecue grill, about 8 inches from the heat source. Grill, turning every 15 minutes, for about 60 minutes or until fork can be inserted into chicken with ease and no pink remains. During last 30 minutes of grilling, brush generously with marinade. (Be sure to discard bay leaf and excess marinade.)

Eye-Opener Lemon-Coconut Chicken

4 to 6 servings

This isn't everyday fried chicken. It's an oven-fried version that has some real pizzazz.

4 tablespoons
(¼ cup) butter or
margarine, melted

2 eggs

1 can (3½ ounces)
flaked coconut

¾ cup finely crushed
wheat-cracker
crumbs

1 teaspoon grated
fresh lemon peel

½ teaspoon salt

½ teaspoon ground
ginger

1 3- to 4-pound
chicken, cut into
8 pieces

Preheat oven to 375°F. Melt the butter in a 9"x13" baking dish. In a shallow bowl, beat the eggs with a fork. In another shallow bowl, mix together the coconut, cracker crumbs, lemon peel, salt, and ginger. Dip the chicken, one piece at a time, in the beaten eggs, then in cracker crumb mixture to coat. Arrange chicken in a single layer in the baking dish. Bake for about 1 hour, turning occasionally, until chicken is done and fork can be inserted into thickest part of chicken with ease.

Baja Barbecued Chicken

4 servings

This has a barbecue taste from a Mexican-Caribbean combination that's a lip-smacking sensation. Try saying that fast—well, you'll say it when you taste it.

2 pounds chicken drumsticks and/or thighs

SAUCE

1 can (8 ounces) tomato sauce

¼ cup light molasses

3 tablespoons Worcestershire sauce

1 tablespoon instant minced onion

1 tablespoon lemon juice

½ teaspoon chili powder

Preheat oven to 350°F. Place the chicken on broiler pan; bake for 30 minutes. Meanwhile, combine all the sauce ingredients in a small bowl. Turn heat to broil and broil chicken for 20 to 25 minutes, turning frequently. During the last 15 minutes of broiling, brush the chicken several times with sauce.

Chicken Salad Pitas

10 sandwiches

Ever forget to buy bread or fillings for the family's lunch boxes? Never again! Just freeze these great-tasting treats and have them ready whenever they're needed.

3 tablespoons Worcestershire sauce

3 tablespoons white wine vinegar

½ teaspoon sugar

1 teaspoon salt

¼ teaspoon pepper

3 tablespoons vegetable oil

2 small green or red bell peppers, cut into thin strips

½ cup coarsely chopped onion

2 cups diced cooked chicken

1 cup canned chick peas (garbanzo beans), drained

5 6-inch pita breads, each cut in half

Butter or margarine, at room temperature

In a small bowl, combine the Worcestershire sauce, vinegar, sugar, salt, and pepper. In a medium-sized skillet, heat the oil over medium heat. Cook the peppers and onion for 5 minutes, or until peppers are crisp-tender. Remove from heat. Add the chicken and chick peas. Add Worcestershire mixture and toss until well coated. Spread inside of pita halves with butter and fill with chicken mixture. Serve immediately, or freeze if desired.

NOTE: To freeze, place sandwiches in individual sandwich bags. Sandwiches may be kept frozen for 2 weeks. Allow 2 to 3 hours to thaw. Great for school lunches—from freezer to lunchbox to tummy in just about the right amount of time!

Herbed Chicken

4 to 6 servings

Gonna be real busy tomorrow? Wanna get a jump on things? Prepare this dish tonight and just reheat it in a low oven for 20 minutes. Instant hero—hooray!

- ½ cup all-purpose flour
- ½ cup fine, dry bread crumbs
- 1 teaspoon paprika
- 1 teaspoon salt
- ¼ teaspoon pepper
- ¼ teaspoon ground thyme

- 1 3- to 4-pound chicken, cut into 8 pieces
- 4 tablespoons (¼ cup) butter or margarine, melted
- 1 tablespoon vegetable oil

Preheat oven to 400°F. Put the flour, bread crumbs, and seasonings in a plastic or paper bag; shake to mix. Add 2 or 3 chicken pieces to bag; shake well to coat, and remove. Repeat with remaining chicken. Pour the melted butter and oil into a 9"x13" baking dish; add chicken pieces. Bake, uncovered, for 30 minutes. Reduce heat to 350°F, turn chicken pieces over, and bake for an additional 20 to 25 minutes or until tender.

Oven-Fried Chicken with Honey Butter Sauce

4 to 6 servings

Pure Southern hospitality on a platter! Try this once and you'll be using it as a kitchen standard from then on.

1 cup all-purpose flour

2 teaspoons salt

¼ teaspoon pepper

2 teaspoons paprika

1 3- to 4-pound chicken, cut into 8 pieces

8 tablespoons (1 stick) butter or margarine, melted

HONEY BUTTER SAUCE

4 tablespoons (¼ cup) butter

¼ cup honey

¼ cup lemon juice

Preheat oven to 400°F. Combine the flour, salt, pepper, and paprika in a shallow bowl. Dredge chicken pieces in flour mixture. Pour the melted butter into a 9"x13" baking pan. Add pieces of floured chicken in a single layer, turning chicken to coat with butter. Bake skin-side down for 30 minutes. While chicken is cooking, make sauce by melting the butter in a small pan and beating in the honey and lemon juice. Turn chicken pieces, pour Honey Butter Sauce over, and bake for an additional 30 minutes or until tender. Spoon pan juices over chicken and serve.

Special Easy Chicken

4 to 6 servings

Really easy, really homey. I sometimes use wine instead of the chicken broth to give it a little different taste; you can even use just water if you don't have broth.

1 3- to 4-pound chicken, cut into 8 pieces

All-purpose flour, seasoned with salt, pepper, and paprika, for dredging

3 tablespoons butter or margarine

3 tablespoons vegetable oil

½ cup chopped onion

2 cans (15½ ounces each) black-eyed peas, undrained

½ cup chicken broth

½ teaspoon dried oregano, tarragon, or thyme

1 medium-sized fresh tomato, chopped

Lightly dredge the chicken in the seasoned flour. Heat the butter and oil in a large Dutch oven or 2 large skillets and cook chicken over medium heat, turning, until golden brown. Remove chicken and keep warm. Sauté the onion in the Dutch oven (or one of the skillets) for about 5 minutes or until tender. Add remaining ingredients except tomato, and bring to a boil. Add chicken pieces to the pan, pressing chicken down into the peas, and sprinkle the tomato over the top. Cover and simmer for 35 to 40 minutes or until chicken is fork-tender.

Chicken Pecan Skillet

4 to 6 servings

A great brunch or lunch dish that's just right for holiday time or any time.

⅓ cup finely chopped celery

2 tablespoons chopped scallions

6 tablespoons butter or margarine

⅔ cup water

2 cups herb-seasoned stuffing mix

1 tablespoon vegetable oil

3 eggs, beaten

1 can (5 ounces) evaporated milk

½ cup chopped pecans

2½ cups diced cooked chicken

1 cup (4 ounces) grated Swiss cheese

Chopped fresh parsley for garnish

In a large skillet, sauté the celery and scallions in the butter. Stir in the water and stuffing mix; set aside. Heat oil in a large skillet. In a medium-sized bowl, combine the eggs, evaporated milk, ¼ cup of the pecans, and the chicken. Pour into heated skillet and sprinkle evenly with the Swiss cheese. Cover with stuffing mixture and sprinkle remaining pecans over top. Cook over medium-low heat for 10 to 15 minutes, until set. Sprinkle with chopped parsley before serving.

Spanish-Style Chicken

4 to 6 servings

*Here's a quick favorite of mine: I change it each time I
make it by adding ½ teaspoon dried rosemary one time,
basil the next, then thyme, tarragon, or oregano, and so
on and so on. . . .*

- ⅓ cup olive or vegetable oil
- 3 to 4 pounds chicken parts
- 1 cup dry white wine
- 1 cup minced fresh parsley
- 1 to 2 tablespoons minced fresh garlic
- 1 bay leaf
- Salt and pepper to taste

Heat the oil in a large skillet. Sauté the chicken, turning,
for about 5 minutes, or until golden on all sides. Add all
remaining ingredients and bring to a boil. Reduce heat
and simmer, uncovered, about 35 to 40 minutes, until
chicken is tender. Remove bay leaf before serving.

NOTE: You may buy a whole chicken and cut it into pieces,
or buy only your favorite parts. I prefer thighs, but I tend to
serve breasts when cooking for company. Breasts alone do not
take as long to cook, so adjust the time accordingly.

Island Turkey Supper

4 to 6 servings

Capture the taste of the Caribbean with this easy "throw-together." There are many good brands of precooked turkey available in the markets now, so you don't even have to roast a turkey if you don't want to. But you know those leftover turkey scraps that we can hardly do anything with? They sure turn out perfect this way.

3 cups cooked white rice

1 teaspoon curry powder

2 cups diced cooked turkey

2 tablespoons finely chopped onion

6 to 8 stuffed green olives, sliced

1 can (10¾ ounces) condensed cream of mushroom soup

½ cup milk

½ cup (2 ounces) shredded Cheddar cheese

Preheat oven to 350°F. Mix the rice and curry powder, and spread over the bottom of a greased 9-inch square baking dish. Cover evenly with the turkey, onion, and olives. Combine the soup and milk; pour over turkey mixture. Top with cheese. Bake for 25 to 30 minutes until cheese is melted.

Tropical Barbecued Chicken

4 to 6 servings

For a real tropical adventure I finish this on the grill and garnish it with pineapple, papaya, and red pepper slices. That way it looks and tastes Caribbean.

1 3- to 4-pound chicken, quartered

Vegetable oil

1 can (20 ounces) pineapple slices in natural juice, drained and juice reserved

Pineapple for garnish

Papaya for garnish

Red pepper slices for garnish

SAUCE

2 cups mild barbecue sauce

¾ cup reserved pineapple juice

½ teaspoon ground ginger

½ teaspoon ground cinnamon

Dash ground cloves

Preheat oven to 400°F. Coat the chicken pieces with oil. Arrange chicken in a single layer in a greased 9"x13" baking dish. Bake chicken for 15 to 20 minutes. Remove chicken from oven. Arrange the pineapple slices over chicken. Combine all sauce ingredients; pour sauce over chicken. Cover chicken and bake for 25 minutes. Uncover and bake for an additional 20 to 25 minutes, until chicken is cooked through and golden brown.

NOTE: Serve chicken over rice with its sauce and the garnishes.

California Chili Chicken

6 to 8 servings

When you need something right away, try this fast chili for one of today's light meals with more than a light taste. Did I say fast? Super fast! Plus, it's super served with cheese nachos. Mmmm . . . mmmm!

- 2 cans (29 ounces each) tomato sauce
- 1 cup finely chopped onion
- 2 to 3 tablespoons chili powder (to taste)
- 1 teaspoon salt
- ½ teaspoon ground ginger
- 1 teaspoon grated orange rind
- 1 teaspoon dried oregano
- 3 pounds boneless chicken (white or dark meat), cut into ½-inch cubes
- 2 cans (1 pound each) red kidney beans

Combine the tomato sauce, onion, chili powder, salt, ginger, orange rind, and oregano in a large saucepan. Bring to a boil. Add the chicken. Reduce heat and cook, stirring occasionally with a wooden spoon, no longer than 7 to 8 minutes. Add the kidney beans, stir gently, and cook just until warmed through.

NOTE: Serve over rice or cheese nacho chips. I always put in at least a half teaspoon of hot pepper sauce—it's delicious, but it's up to you.

Chicken Dinner, Camp-Style

4 to 6 servings

This is a perfect time-saver 'cause it's a one-pan throw-together that tastes as if you must have stood over the stove all day long. Ha! No chance! You can make it Creole-style by adding hot pepper sauce or cacciatore-style by adding oregano and garlic. With a few different seasonings you've got a new dish every time and it's still just as easy.

1 3- to 4-pound chicken, cut into 8 pieces

1 tablespoon vegetable oil

1¾ cups water

1 can (6 ounces) tomato paste

1 envelope (1.5 ounces) spaghetti sauce mix

1 can (4 ounces) mushroom pieces, undrained

4 potatoes, quartered

1 green bell pepper, coarsely chopped

In a large skillet, brown the chicken in the oil. Pour off grease. Add the water, tomato paste, and sauce mix; stir until smooth. Stir in the mushrooms and potatoes. Cover and simmer for 20 minutes. Stir in the green pepper; cover and simmer for 10 to 15 minutes more or until chicken and vegetables are tender.

F rench Chicken

4 servings

Everybody thinks French cooking is so fancy and difficult. I won't tell them how really easy it is if you don't! This is simply baked chicken made "French gourmet" by way of the tarragon, parsley, and garlic—couldn't be easier.

1 **3- to 4-pound chicken**

1 **garlic clove, peeled and halved**

   Fresh ground pepper to taste

4 **tablespoons (¼ cup) butter or margarine**

1 **tablespoon dried tarragon**

1 **tablespoon chopped fresh parsley**

Preheat oven to 350°F. Trim excess skin and fat from chicken. Rub chicken all over with garlic; lightly sprinkle with pepper. Place chicken, breast-side up, on a rack in a shallow roasting pan. In a small saucepan, melt butter; stir in tarragon and parsley. Bake chicken for 1½ to 1¾ hours or until done and golden brown, basting with herb mixture every 15 minutes. Juices should run clear when chicken is pricked with a fork.

Turkey Cacciatore

2 servings

Looking for a change of pace? How about making turkey cacciatore—it's today's lightness with yesterday's taste. And if you thought nothing was easier than chicken cacciatore, just try it with turkey.

- 2 turkey wings
  Salt and pepper to taste
- ½ cup chopped onion
- 1 cup sliced fresh mushrooms (optional)
- 1 garlic clove, minced
- 1 green bell pepper, sliced

- 1 cup dry white wine or water
- 2 cups chopped canned tomatoes
- 1 tablespoon chopped fresh parsley
- 1 teaspoon dried oregano (optional)

Preheat broiler. Split the wings at each joint and discard tips. Broil the wings, turning, until evenly browned. (You can also brown the wings on an outdoor grill.) Combine all the remaining ingredients in a nonstick Dutch oven; add wings. Cover and simmer over low heat, stirring occasionally, for about 1 hour, or until turkey is quite tender. Uncover and cook for about 15 to 20 minutes more, until sauce is thick. Spoon sauce over wings and serve.

NOTE: Serve with pasta and you can't go wrong.

Mexican Seasoned Chicken Croissants

6 sandwiches

These are just too good to be easy, but they are. And so rich tasting! Wait 'til you serve these at a brunch or lunch.

3 cups cubed cooked chicken

1 cup (8 ounces) sour cream

3 scallions, finely chopped

2 tablespoons finely chopped green bell pepper

1 tablespoon lime juice

1 teaspoon ground cumin

¼ teaspoon garlic powder

¼ teaspoon cayenne pepper

6 croissants

In a large bowl, mix the chicken and all other ingredients except croissants. Cover and refrigerate for at least 1 hour to "marry" the flavors. Preheat oven to 350°F. Slice croissants in half lengthwise and pull out the insides of the bottom halves. Fill croissant bottoms with chicken mixture and cover with croissant tops. Set croissants on a cookie sheet and place in the oven for about 15 minutes to warm through.

NOTE: If you'd like, top chicken with cheese and place under the broiler to melt the cheese. I like to serve them with a side of salsa, and sometimes I even put a little salsa or some bottled sauce right on the melted cheese.

Special Chicken Salad

about 3 cups (enough for 4 sandwiches)

When you have chicken salad on hand, you're ready for anything. Usually we chop some chicken, add some celery and mayo, and that's it. Well, this one with a few added items really raises those eyebrows.

½ cup mayonnaise

1 tablespoon Dijon mustard

1 tablespoon lemon juice

2 medium-sized garlic cloves, minced

2 cups chopped cooked chicken

½ cup chopped red bell pepper

¼ cup chopped scallions

½ cup chopped carrots (optional)

In a large bowl, combine the mayonnaise, mustard, lemon juice, and garlic; mix well. Add the chicken, red pepper, scallions and carrots; mix gently.

NOTE: This salad is great on whole-wheat toast, croissants, or your favorite bread. (Handy-to-hold pitas are *my* favorite for this.)

Baked Crispy Chicken

4 to 6 servings

An easy-to-do recipe that can be used for either company or the home folks. And they won't get this taste from a take-out place, 'cause it's yours alone.

1 egg, slightly beaten

5 tablespoons cider vinegar

1 tablespoon Worcestershire sauce

2 teaspoons hot pepper sauce

1½ teaspoons onion salt

½ teaspoon celery salt

1 3- to 4-pound chicken, cut into 8 pieces

2 tablespoons butter or margarine

Instant mashed potato flakes for coating

In a small bowl, combine the egg, vinegar, Worcestershire sauce, hot pepper sauce, and onion and celery salts. Put the chicken pieces in a large bowl and pour vinegar mixture over. Marinate for several hours or overnight in the refrigerator, turning chicken several times. After marinating, preheat oven to 400°F. Melt butter in a large shallow baking dish. Put potato flakes in a shallow dish and roll chicken pieces in flakes until well coated. Place chicken pieces skin-side down, 1 to 2 inches apart, in baking dish and bake for 25 minutes. Turn chicken pieces and bake for 20 to 30 minutes longer or until chicken is cooked through.

MEATS

T he "something to bite into," the meal "feature"—gotta have a main course that's gang-busters! Because when everybody asks, "What are they serving?" they mean the main course, and most people to-day still want the "big four"—beef, veal, pork, and lamb. But, as with everything else in this book, easy doesn't mean less good. Nope! In fact, easy probably means less played with. Remember when you'd warm that pot roast or stew the second time? Could it be any simpler to get that much flavor? Doesn't have to be expensive either. Better to be easy, quick, sensible, and TASTY—then it'll be a complete **OOH it's so GOOD!!**™

Timetable for Roasting
Large Beef Roasts

To roast beef roasts: Place beef roast, straight from the refrigerator, fat-side up (if present) on a rack in a shallow roasting pan. Rub with herbs or season, if desired. Insert meat thermometer so the tip is centered in the roast but does not touch bone or fat. Always roast without a cover or the addition of liquid, otherwise the meat will be braised. Remove the roast from the oven when the thermometer registers 10 degrees F. lower than desired; the roast will continue to cook as it stands. Allowing the roast to "stand" for 15 to 20 minutes after roasting makes carving easier.

Cut	Approximate Weight (in pounds)	Oven Temperature (in degrees F.)	Final Meat Thermometer Reading (in degrees F.)	Approximate Cooking Time* (minutes per pound)
Beef Rib Roast	8 to 10	300 to 325	140 (rare) 160 (medium)	19 to 21 23 to 25
Beef Rib Eye Roast	8 to 10	350	140 (rare) 160 (medium)	13 to 15 16 to 18
Beef Tenderloin Roast, Whole	4 to 6	425	140 (rare)	45 to 60 (total cooking time)
Beef Round Tip Roast	8 to 10	300 to 325	140 (rare) 160 (medium)	18 to 22 23 to 25
Beef Top Round Roast	6 to 10	300 to 325	140 (rare) 160 (medium)	17 to 19 22 to 24
Beef Top Loin Roast	7 to 9	300 to 325	140 (rare) 160 (medium)	9 to 11 13 to 15

* Cooking times are based on meat taken directly from the refrigerator.

Courtesy of the Meat Board Test Kitchens

Timetable for Roasting Veal

Roasting is the simplest cooking method because it requires so little attention. It is most appropriate for larger cuts of veal from the loin, sirloin, and rib. A boneless veal shoulder arm, eye round, or rump roast also can be roasted successfully in a slow oven (300° to 325°F.).

A shallow roasting pan with rack and a meat thermometer are the only equipment needed for roasting.

To roast veal: Place roast (straight from refrigerator), fat-side up, on rack in open roasting pan. Season either before or after cooking. Insert meat thermometer into thickest part of roast, not touching bone or fat. Do not add water. Do not cover. Roast in slow oven (300° to 325°F.) to 5 degrees below desired doneness. (Oven does not have to be preheated.) Allow roast to stand for 15 to 20 minutes before serving. Temperature will rise about 5 degrees, and roast will be easier to carve.

Roasting at 300° to 325°F.

Cut	Approximate Weight (in pounds)	Final Meat Thermometer Reading (in degrees F.)	Approximate Cooking Time* (minutes per pound)
Loin	3 to 4	160 (medium)	34 to 36
		170 (well)	38 to 40
Loin (boneless)	2 to 3	160 (medium)	18 to 20
		170 (well)	22 to 24
Rib	4 to 5	160 (medium)	25 to 27
		170 (well)	29 to 31
Crown (12 to 14 ribs)	7½ to 9½	160 (medium)	19 to 21
		170 (well)	21 to 23
Rib Eye	2 to 3	160 (medium)	26 to 28
		170 (well)	30 to 33
Rump (boneless)	2 to 3	160 (medium)	33 to 35
		170 (well)	37 to 40
Shoulder (boneless)	2½ to 3	160 (medium)	31 to 34
		170 (well)	34 to 37

* Cooking times are based on meat taken directly from the refrigerator.

Courtesy of the Beef Board and Veal Committee of the Beef Industry Council

Timetable for Roasting Pork

To roast pork: Place pork, fat-side up, on rack in open roasting pan. Rub with herbs or season, if desired. Insert meat thermometer so bulb is centered in roast but does not touch bone or fat. Do not add water. Do not cover. Roast in slow oven (300° to 325°F.), unless instructed otherwise, to 5 degrees below recommended degree of doneness. (Roast continues cooking after removal from oven.) Cover roast with foil tent and let stand for 15 to 20 minutes before carving.

Cut	Approximate Weight (in pounds)	Oven Temperature (in degrees F.)	Final Meat Thermometer Reading (in degrees F.)	Approximate Cooking Time (minutes per pound)
Loin, Center (bone in)	3 to 5	325	160 (medium) 170 (well)	20 to 25 26 to 31
Blade Loin/ Sirloin (boneless, tied)	2½ to 3½	325	170 (well)	33 to 38
Boneless Rib End—Chef's Prime™	2 to 4	325	160 (medium) 170 (well)	26 to 31 28 to 33
Top (double)	3 to 4	325	160 (medium) 170 (well)	29 to 34 33 to 38
Top	2 to 4	325	160 (medium) 170 (well)	23 to 33 30 to 40
Crown	6 to 10	325	170 (well)	20 to 25
Leg				
Whole (bone in)	12	325	170 (well)	23 to 25
Top (inside)	3½	325	170 (well)	38 to 42
Bottom (outside)	3½	325	170 (well)	40 to 45
Blade Boston (boneless)	3 to 4	325	170 (well)	40 to 45

Cut	Approximate Size	Oven Temperature (in degrees F.)	Final Meat Thermometer Reading (in degrees F.) or Gauge	Total Cooking Time* (in minutes)
Tenderloin	½ to 1 pound	425	160 (medium) 170 (well)	27 to 29 30 to 32
Backribs	——	425	tender	1½ to 1¾ hrs.
Country-style Ribs	1″ slices	425	tender	1½ to 1¾ hrs.
Spareribs	——	425	tender	1½ to 1¾ hrs.
Ground Pork Loaf	1 to 1½ pounds	350	170 (well)	55 to 65
Meatballs	1″ 2″	350 350	170 (well) 170 (well)	25 to 30 30 to 35

Note: Smaller roasts require more minutes per pound than larger roasts. Cooking times are based on meat taken directly from the refrigerator.

Courtesy of the Meat Board Test Kitchens & Pork Industry Group

Timetable for Roasting Lamb

To roast lamb: Place lamb, fat-side up, on rack in open roasting pan. Insert meat thermometer so bulb is centered in roast and not touching bone or fat. Do not add water. Do not cover. Roast in slow oven (300° to 325°F.) to desired degree of doneness. Season with salt and pepper if desired.

Roasting at 325°F.

Cut	Approximate Weight (in pounds)	Final Meat Thermometer Reading (in degrees F.)	Approximate Cooking Time* (minutes per pound)
Leg	7 to 9	140 (rare) 160 (medium) 170 (well)	15 to 20 20 to 25 25 to 30
Leg	5 to 7	140 (rare) 160 (medium) 170 (well)	20 to 25 25 to 30 30 to 35
Leg (boneless)	4 to 7	140 (rare) 160 (medium) 170 (well)	25 to 30 30 to 35 35 to 40
Leg, Shank Half	3 to 4	140 (rare) 160 (medium) 170 (well)	30 to 35 40 to 45 45 to 50
Leg, Sirloin Half	3 to 4	140 (rare) 160 (medium) 170 (well)	25 to 30 35 to 40 45 to 50
Shoulder† (boneless)	3½ to 5	140 (rare) 160 (medium) 170 (well)	30 to 35 35 to 40 40 to 45

Note: Cooking times are based on meat taken directly from the refrigerator.
* Oven not preheated.
† For presliced, bone-in shoulder, add 5 minutes per pound to times recommended for boneless shoulder.

Courtesy of the Lamb Committee of the National Live Stock & Meat Board.

inter Beef Stew

6 servings

Nothing can take the chill out of winter like a hearty beef stew. For something a little different, try veal or lamb stew meat here instead of beef. The nicest part is that there are no rules; a little bit more or less of most of these ingredients is perfectly fine. So is adding another type of veggie you've got hanging around in the refrigerator. Sure! Go ahead and throw it in. It'll work fine. Have fun!

- 2 pounds stew beef
- 2 tablespoons all-purpose flour
- 3 tablespoons vegetable oil
- 1 teaspoon salt (optional)
- ½ teaspoon pepper
- 3 cups water

- 2 envelopes (1.25 ounces each) dried onion soup mix
- 3 large onions, quartered
- 8 carrots, cut into 1-inch chunks
- 6 medium-sized potatoes, peeled and quartered

Dredge the beef in the flour. In a Dutch oven, heat the oil, add beef, and brown it on all sides. Add the salt, pepper, water, and onion soup mix; bring to a boil. Simmer, covered, for 1½ hours, or until the meat is almost tender. Add the vegetables and simmer, stirring occasionally, for another 45 minutes or until meat and vegetables are tender.

Grilled Meat Loaf

6 to 8 servings

This is a new and exciting way to prepare an old favorite and still take advantage of grilling outside. (And no heating up the kitchen in warm weather!)

- 2 pounds lean ground beef
- ½ cup dry bread crumbs
- 2 eggs
- 2 tablespoons instant minced onions
- 1 tablespoon prepared mustard
- 2 teaspoons Worcestershire sauce
- ½ cup ketchup
- ½ teaspoon salt
- ¼ teaspoon pepper

GLAZE

- ¼ cup ketchup or chili sauce
- 1 tablespoon maple-flavored syrup or brown sugar
- 1 tablespoon vegetable oil
- 1 teaspoon Worcestershire sauce

In a small bowl, combine all the glaze ingredients. In a large bowl, combine all the remaining ingredients; mix well. On a double thickness of heavy-duty aluminum foil, shape mixture into a loaf. Fold sides of foil up to form a "pan." Brush the glaze over the meat loaf. Place the meat loaf, in its foil pan, on grill over medium-hot coals. Cover with hood of grill or aluminum foil tent. Cook for 30 to 40 minutes, brushing occasionally with glaze, until no pink remains in center of loaf.

Deviled Beef Rolls

4 servings

This is just like the taste of Steak Diane—maybe better—and just as fancy-looking, but it's easier to make and easier to serve. In fact, this is now my standard way to get the Steak Diane taste.

2 tablespoons dried onion soup mix

4 teaspoons water

3 tablespoons Dijon mustard

4 cube steaks (approximately 6 ounces each)

Dash pepper

1 can (4 ounces) sliced mushrooms, drained

2 tablespoons butter or margarine, melted

Preheat broiler. In a small bowl, mix the dry soup mix and water; let stand for 5 minutes. Stir in the mustard. Sprinkle the steaks with pepper and spread the mustard mixture over one side of each steak. Arrange sliced mushrooms on top. Roll up each steak and fasten with a wooden toothpick. Brush with some of the melted butter. Place rolls on broiling pan and broil 4 to 5 inches from heat source for 5 to 6 minutes. Turn rolls over and brush with remaining butter; broil for 5 or 6 minutes more. Remove toothpicks and serve.

Oriental Steak

4 to 6 servings

You'll think this came from your favorite Oriental restaurant. And substitutions are fine because using your own touches makes it extra special.

- 1 2½- to 3-pound steak (flank, chuck, sirloin, or round)
- 2 tablespoons bottled browning and seasoning sauce

MARINADE
- ½ cup soy sauce
- 2 tablespoons honey
- 2 tablespoons cider vinegar
- 2 tablespoons sesame oil
- ¼ teaspoon ground ginger
- 2 garlic cloves, minced

In a small bowl, combine all the marinade ingredients. Put the steak into a plastic bag, pour in the marinade, tie the bag securely, and set in a shallow baking pan. Let marinate in the refrigerator for at least 3 to 4 hours or overnight. After marinating, preheat broiler. Remove steak from the bag (discarding marinade) and place on broiling pan. Brush with the browning and seasoning sauce. Broil, turning once, to your desired degree of doneness.

NOTE: For an easy change of pace, I like to use regular oil instead of sesame oil and bottled garlic instead of fresh, add a few shakes of hot pepper sauce, and try some bottled sweet-and-sour sauce instead of honey.

Cola Roast

8 to 10 servings

Unusual, to say the least! But using the cola does so much to make the flavor old-fashioned rich. You'll see how easy pot roast can really be with this one. And when you tell them what you made it with, they'll be all ears. Oh, yeah— make enough for seconds.

1 teaspoon salt

½ teaspoon pepper

½ teaspoon garlic powder

1 4- to 5-pound bottom round roast

3 tablespoons vegetable oil

1 can (12 ounces) cola-flavored carbonated beverage

12 ounces chili sauce

2 tablespoons Worcestershire sauce

2 tablespoons hot pepper sauce

Preheat oven to 325°F. In a small bowl, combine the salt, pepper, and garlic powder; rub over surface of roast. In a Dutch oven, heat the oil to hot and brown roast on all sides. Transfer roast to roasting pan. Combine all the remaining ingredients; pour over roast. Cover and roast for 2½ to 3 hours or until tender.

asy Chili

8 to 10 servings

Here's a delicious chili that lets you add your own special touches—like using cube beef instead of hamburger or maybe adding fresh peppers.

- 3 tablespoons vegetable oil
- 5 pounds ground beef
- 1 large onion, diced
- 1 tablespoon finely chopped garlic
- 1 can (28 ounces) whole tomatoes
- 3 cups barbecue sauce
- 3 tablespoons chili powder

- 1 tablespoon salt
- 1 tablespoon hot pepper sauce
- 1 tablespoon cumin
- 4 cans (15½ ounces each) kidney beans
- Tortilla chips (optional)
- Jalapeño peppers (optional)

In a large, heavy skillet or Dutch oven, heat the oil. Add the meat, onion, and garlic, and cook, stirring, over medium-high heat until meat is browned. Add the tomatoes, barbecue sauce, chili powder, salt, hot pepper sauce, cumin, and kidney beans; stir to mix well. Cover and simmer for an hour, stirring occasionally. Serve with warm tortilla chips and a side dish of jalapeño peppers, if desired.

NOTE: You can add ½ cup of instant potatoes for the last 10 minutes of cooking to thicken this, if you like. Chili tastes best made a day ahead and reheated.

Barbecued Beef Sandwiches

8 to 12 sandwiches

It's like an old-fashioned Southern pork or beef pull. Put it on buns and boy, oh boy—will they love it! There's no fussing 'cause you just pile it on.

1 2½- to 3-pound beef roast (round, shoulder, or brisket)

Hamburger buns

SAUCE

1 cup ketchup

1 can (12 ounces) beer

1 envelope (1.25 ounces) dried onion soup mix

Preheat oven to 250°F. In a medium-sized bowl, mix together all the sauce ingredients. Place roast in a roasting pan. Pour the sauce over the roast and cook for 4 to 4½ hours. (Roast can also be cooked in a crockpot on low.) Meat is done when it is so tender it can be pulled apart with a fork into shreds or pieces. Place shredded beef on buns and serve.

NOTE: I like to serve these with any good bottled barbecue sauce poured on top.

Goulash Stew

about 4 servings

*With sour cream and paprika it's Hungarian. With cara-
way seeds it's German. With tarragon it's French. With
cumin it's Mexican. And with any of them it tastes even
better reheated the next day. It's a great "make-ahead"
dish so there's no fuss at dinner time.*

3½ cups water

2 pounds stew beef

1 large onion, diced

1 large potato,
   peeled and cut into
   1½-inch cubes

1½ cups ketchup

¼ cup Worcester-
   shire sauce

2 tablespoons firmly
   packed brown
   sugar

1 tablespoon salt
   (optional)

1 tablespoon
   paprika (or hot
   paprika, if you
   want it truly
   Hungarian-style)

¼ teaspoon dry
   mustard

3 tablespoons
   all-purpose flour

In a large pot, combine 3 cups water and all other ingredients except flour. Bring to a boil, reduce heat, and simmer for 2 hours. In a small bowl, mix flour and remaining
½ cup water until smooth. Return stew to a full boil and
gradually whisk in the flour-water mixture. Mix and cook
until stew juices start to thicken.

NOTE: Serve over noodles.

Applesauce Meat Loaf

3 to 4 servings

Here's how you can take that tired old meat loaf and turn it into a real treat by making it sort of German-style with a tang of freshness (that's what the applesauce does).

1½ pounds ground beef

¾ cup dry bread crumbs

1 egg

½ cup applesauce

1 small onion, finely chopped, or 1½ teaspoons instant minced onion

1 teaspoon salt

Pinch pepper

2 tablespoons chili sauce

Preheat oven to 350°F. In a large bowl, thoroughly mix all ingredients except chili sauce. Place mixture in a greased 9"x5" loaf pan and bake for 30 minutes. Spread the chili sauce over the top of the loaf; return it to the oven and bake for an additional 30 minutes, until no pink remains in center. Serve hot or cold.

NOTE: This mixture can also be shaped into meatballs and simmered in a favorite tomato sauce or meat gravy. Serve with pasta, rice, or potatoes.

Beef Short Ribs Supreme

4 to 6 servings

Here's a sweet-and-sour short ribs dinner that tastes like Momma's, especially if you make it a day ahead and then just heat it up before dinner. (The cooling also allows the fat to rise to the top of the sauce and solidify. Then you can remove it, reheat the ribs, and enjoy much leaner, more delicious ribs than you've had in a long time.)

- 3 pounds beef short ribs
- ½ cup chopped onion
- 1 garlic clove, minced
- 1 can (6 ounces) tomato paste
- 1 cup ketchup
- ¾ cup firmly packed brown sugar
- ½ cup white vinegar
- ½ cup water
- 2 tablespoons prepared mustard
- 2 teaspoons salt

In a Dutch oven, over medium-high heat, brown ribs on all sides. (You do not need to use any oil or shortening.) Reduce heat to low, cover, and cook for 1 hour. Drain off grease. Combine all the remaining ingredients, and pour over ribs. Cover and cook for 1½ hours longer, or until meat is tender.

NOTE: You can substitute a 3-pound chuck roast for the ribs and it will still taste great.

Cottage Pie

4 servings

This is stick-to-the-ribs delicious and satisfying. Makes you feel warm and cozy on a cold winter night.

- 6 tablespoons butter
- 1 cup diced onion
- 1½ pounds lean ground beef
- Salt and pepper to taste
- ¼ teaspoon dried savory
- 1 cup (8 ounces) canned or bottled brown gravy
- 2 cups mashed potatoes

Preheat oven to 400°F. Heat 4 tablespoons butter in a large skillet. Add the onion and cook, stirring frequently, until lightly browned. Add the beef, salt, pepper, and savory and cook for 5 minutes. Stir in the gravy and heat until bubbling. Spoon mixture into a greased 2-quart casserole dish. Spread mashed potatoes over top of meat and dot with pieces of butter. Bake for 15 to 20 minutes or until potatoes are lightly browned.

Sweet-and-Sour Beef Brisket

10 to 12 servings

A little sweet, a little sour, all delicious! And convenient too, 'cause you can make it up to 4 or 5 days in advance.

- 1 tablespoon salt
- ½ tablespoon pepper
- 1 garlic clove, minced
- 1 tablespoon paprika
- 1 6- to 7-pound single-cut beef brisket, well trimmed
- ⅓ cup firmly packed brown sugar
- 2 tablespoons white vinegar
- ½ cup ketchup
- 1 onion, thinly sliced

Preheat oven to 350°F. Combine the salt, pepper, garlic, and paprika. Rub brisket all over with mixture and place in a roasting pan. Mix the brown sugar, vinegar, and ketchup in a small bowl; pour over brisket. Lay the onion slices on top of meat. Cover with foil and bake for 3 to 3½ hours, or until tender. Slice brisket diagonally across the grain into thin slices, pour pan juices over, and serve. (If you wish to serve at a later date, you can store the cooked brisket in the refrigerator for up to 4 or 5 days. Just be sure to let the meat cool slightly before refrigerating. Before serving, cover meat with foil and place in a 350°F. oven for 45 minutes or until heated through.)

Veal Scallopini

4 to 6 servings

Here's my version of an Italian classic. Try adding either mushrooms or tomatoes, or both—you'll have everyone thinking you're a gourmet chef.

2 pounds veal cutlets, pounded to about ¼-inch thick and cut into medallions

1 teaspoon salt

⅛ teaspoon pepper

1 cup Marsala wine or sherry

½ cup all-purpose flour

8 tablespoons (1 stick) butter or margarine

1 cup chicken or beef broth

Juice of ½ lemon

1 teaspoon oregano

½ pound fresh mushrooms, sliced (optional)

1 can (16 ounces) whole tomatoes, drained (optional)

Season the medallions with the salt and pepper and place them in a shallow bowl. Pour the wine over the medallions and marinate, covered, in the refrigerator for at least 1 hour but no longer than 1½ hours. Remove veal, reserving the wine. Dredge medallions in the flour. Heat the butter in a large skillet and brown the veal on both sides in batches. Return all the medallions to the skillet and add the broth, lemon juice, reserved wine, oregano, mushrooms, and tomatoes. Simmer for 8 to 10 minutes, stirring occasionally.

NOTE: Serve with your favorite pasta.

Special Veal Chops

2 servings

These are lip-smacking good and easy. Your family will love them, and so will your guests.

2 tablespoons white vinegar

½ teaspoon sugar

½ teaspoon pepper

1 to 2 garlic cloves, crushed or 1 teaspoon bottled chopped garlic

4 loin or rib veal chops, about 1 inch thick

MARINADE

½ cup vegetable oil

6 tablespoons soy sauce

6 tablespoons ketchup

Mix all marinade ingredients in a medium-sized bowl. Place the chops in a shallow dish and pour marinade over. Marinate in the refrigerator for 2 to 6 hours (depending on how flavorful you like them). After marinating, preheat broiler. Remove chops from marinade and broil for 10 to 12 minutes. Turn chops over and broil for 5 minutes more, or until done to your liking.

NOTE: You can also use smart-priced shoulder veal chops. Try these chops on the grill, too—they're just as "indoor fancy" and delicious.

Sausage 'n' Egg Casserole

6 to 8 servings

A great brunch idea! Make it your own by varying the cheese or adding crumbled bacon. How about a little hot pepper sauce? Great! Any way at all, it's gonna smell like a farm kitchen at breakfast time.

¾ **pound bulk pork sausage**

10 **eggs**

1 **cup milk**

¾ **teaspoon salt**

1½ **cups (6 ounces) shredded sharp Cheddar cheese**

1½ **cups packaged croutons (garlic- or onion-flavored)**

Preheat oven to 325°F. In a large skillet, brown the sausage over medium heat. Drain off fat. Put sausage in a greased 2-quart casserole dish. In a large bowl, beat the eggs; stir in the milk, salt, and cheese. Pour egg mixture over sausage. Sprinkle with croutons. Bake, uncovered, for 45 to 50 minutes. Let stand for 5 minutes before serving.

Dilled Pork Cutlets

4 servings

Pork, "the other white meat," is such a great buy. And here's how it can so easily be a fancy dish for company, because a little chopped scallion makes it taste like a French country kitchen original—delicate but so full-flavored.

3 tablespoons mayonnaise

2 tablespoons prepared mustard

2 tablespoons lemon juice

2 tablespoons dried dillweed

4 boneless pork loin cutlets, pounded to ¼-inch thick

Flour for dredging

1 tablespoon butter or margarine

Combine the mayonnaise, mustard, lemon juice, and dillweed in a small bowl. Dredge the cutlets in flour. Heat the butter in a large skillet and sauté the cutlets over medium-high heat. Reduce heat to medium, brush cutlets with the mayonnaise mixture, and cook, turning several times and continuing to brush with the mayonnaise mixture, for 8 to 10 minutes, until lightly browned on both sides.

Honey Pecan Pork Cutlets

2 to 3 servings

Tastes like real down-home. I use veal, turkey, or chicken when I want a bit of a change.

1 pound boneless pork loin cutlets, pounded to ¼-inch thick

Flour for dredging

3 tablespoons butter

¼ cup honey

¼ cup chopped pecans

Dredge the cutlets in flour, shaking off excess. Heat 1 tablespoon butter in a heavy skillet over medium heat. Add cutlets and sauté until brown on both sides, about 5 to 6 minutes. Soften the remaining butter and mix it with the honey and pecans; add to skillet and stir gently. Cover and simmer gently for 7 to 8 minutes. Remove cutlets to a serving platter, and spoon any sauce and pecans remaining in the pan over them.

Austrian-Style Smoky Ribs

8 to 10 servings, 2½ quarts sauce

This is my favorite recipe for ribs. It's so easy to make them inside, too, instead of on an outdoor grill.

12 pounds pork spareribs	SAUCE
1 tablespoon garlic powder	1½ quarts mild barbecue sauce
Seasoned salt to taste	1 quart applesauce
Pepper to taste	1 tablespoon liquid smoke
	2 tablespoons caraway seeds

Preheat oven to 325°F. Season the ribs with the garlic powder, seasoned salt, and pepper and place them in large shallow baking pans. Cover with foil and bake for 1 hour. Meanwhile, mix all sauce ingredients in a large saucepan and simmer for 10 to 15 minutes. Brush ribs all over with sauce. Bake, uncovered, for 30 minutes longer. Or, preheat broiler, brush baked ribs with sauce, and broil for 10 to 12 minutes, turning and brushing with sauce once. Serve with any remaining sauce.

NOTE: Liquid smoke can be found in the condiment section of the supermarket.

Baked Lamb Chops

3 servings

Lamb chops are always a special treat. Try them this way—they're delicious! Fancy-looking and fancy-tasting, too!

- 1 cup chopped fresh parsley
- ⅓ cup Dijon or other prepared mustard
- 4 teaspoons crushed wheat bran cereal

- 6 rib lamb chops
- Juice of ½ lemon
- Garlic powder to taste
- Pepper to taste

Preheat oven to 500°F. Combine the parsley, mustard, and bran in a small bowl; mix well. Trim excess fat from the lamb chops. Rub both sides of chops with lemon juice; sprinkle lightly with the garlic powder and pepper. Press parsley mixture firmly onto both sides of chops. Place chops in a 9"x13" baking dish coated with nonstick vegetable spray; bake for 6 to 7 minutes. Reduce heat to 350°F. and bake for 15 minutes more or until chops are done to your liking.

NOTE: You can use less expensive shoulder lamb chops but you will have to cook them longer than rib chops.

Spiced Lamb-Stuffed Peppers

8 servings

Turn stuffed peppers into an exotic gourmet delight by making them in this Middle Eastern fashion. Middle Eastern food is always great for a dinner party because it sounds so exotic. You know, like "Meet me at the Casbah." Go ahead—give it a shot.

8	medium-sized red, yellow, or green bell peppers	1	teaspoon allspice
1½	pounds lean ground lamb	½	teaspoon ground cumin
1	large onion, finely chopped	½	teaspoon ground cinnamon
2	cups cooked white rice	½	teaspoon black pepper
½	cup ketchup	2	eggs, lightly beaten
½	cup raisins		Salt and cayenne pepper to taste

Preheat oven to 375°F. Slice off tops of the peppers and remove seeds. Remove stems and finely chop the pepper tops. Stand the peppers, cut-end up, in a shallow 1½- to 2-quart casserole coated with a nonstick vegetable spray. Heat a large skillet and add the lamb, crumbling it with your fingers. Cook over medium heat, stirring often, until meat is well browned. Add the onion and chopped pepper.

Cook, stirring, until onion is limp; remove from heat and drain off fat. Stir in the rice, ketchup, raisins, allspice, cumin, cinnamon, black pepper, and eggs; blend well. Add salt and cayenne pepper. Fill peppers with rice mixture, packing lightly. Bake for 30 to 40 minutes, until peppers are soft and can be pierced with a fork.

FISH AND SEAFOOD

Everybody wants fish— it's so easy to make 'cause it's adaptable to any seasoning and it cooks in minutes. (All the health institutions have been telling us how healthy it is, too!) From chowders to main courses, it's a true "fast food." And we all want some new ways to make it exciting, so here are some really easy, smart ones.

TIDBIT: One of the most important things to remember about fish is that to keep it moist and tender, it should be cooked no longer than 10 minutes per inch of thickness. Boiled, baked, broiled, any way at all—just 10 minutes per inch. For instance, a piece of fish 1½ inches thick? About 7 to 8 minutes per side will do it. You'll see—moist, tender, and delicious.

Garlic Shrimp

4 to 5 servings

Funny how when we mention garlic and shrimp every-body's eyes light up. Yup! Does it every time, and this one is a snap!

- 2 pounds small shrimp, peeled and deveined
- 2 tablespoons chopped fresh parsley

- 2½ teaspoons plus 1 teaspoon chopped garlic (fresh or bottled)
- ½ cup olive oil

  Salt and pepper to taste

In a medium-sized bowl, toss the shrimp with the parsley and 2½ teaspoons garlic; let sit in refrigerator, covered, for 3 to 4 hours. Remove shrimp from refrigerator; heat olive oil in a large skillet over medium-high heat. Add the shrimp and remaining 1 teaspoon garlic. Cook, stirring constantly, for 4 to 5 minutes, until shrimp are pink and just cooked through. Add salt and pepper to taste.

NOTE: Sometimes I add chopped fresh dill, basil, or scallions to give it a hint of the traditional scampi flavor. Chunks of swordfish, halibut, or imitation crabmeat work just as well if you want a change. This is great served over spaghetti or linguine.

Onion-Baked Catfish

4 to 6 servings

Looking for a new and exciting fish dish? Here's one that's sure to be a pleaser.

6 farm-raised catfish fillets (about 2 pounds), thawed if frozen

1 cup (8 ounces) sour cream

1 cup mayonnaise

1 package (1 ounce) ranch-style salad dressing mix

2 cans (2.8 ounces each) French-fried onion rings

1 lemon or lime, cut into wedges or slices for garnish

Parsley, watercress, or dill sprigs for garnish

Preheat oven to 350°F. Combine the sour cream, mayonnaise, and salad dressing mix in a small bowl. Pour ¾ cup of mixture into a shallow dish. Process the onion rings in a blender or food processor until finely crushed and put on a plate. Dip fillets in sour cream mixture, then in crushed onion rings to coat. Place fish in an ungreased 9"x13" baking dish. Bake for 20 to 25 minutes or until fish flakes easily with a fork. Remove fillets to a warm serving platter. Garnish as desired with lemon or lime slices and greens. Serve with remaining sour cream mixture.

NOTE: Onion rings may be placed in a plastic bag and crushed with a rolling pin instead of using a blender or food processor. Equal amounts of low-fat sour cream and light mayonnaise may be substituted, if desired. If catfish fillets are not available, any white-fleshed fish will work (try cod, haddock, sole, flounder, or perch).

This recipe was a winner in the National Farm-Raised Catfish Cooking Contest.

reamy Fish Fillets

4 to 6 servings

This is a creamy, luxurious, delicate dish that'll have everybody thinking there's a French chef in the kitchen. When they ask where the chef is, just smile!

- 1 cup (8 ounces) sour cream
- ¼ cup grated Parmesan cheese
- 1 tablespoon lemon juice
- 1 hard-boiled egg, peeled and mashed
- ½ teaspoon salt (optional)

- 2 or 3 drops hot pepper sauce (or to taste)
- 1 small tomato, finely chopped
- 1 small onion, finely diced
- 2 pounds white-fleshed fish fillets
- Paprika

Preheat oven to 350° F. Place all ingredients except the fish and paprika in a large bowl. Mix well, mashing the mixture with the back of a spoon to blend into a smooth, creamy mixture. Place the fillets in a single layer in 1 or 2 greased baking dishes. Spoon the sour cream mixture over the fish; sprinkle with paprika. Bake for 20 to 30 minutes, or until fish flakes easily with a fork.

NOTE: You really can use any kind of fish fillets—perch, sole, snapper, cod, or pollack.

Summer-Fancy Fillets

4 servings

Want a new favorite recipe for fish? Here's one I came across that's both new and easy—and fancy-looking, to boot!

2 eggs

2 tablespoons water

Few dashes of hot pepper sauce (to taste)

4 thin white-fleshed fish fillets (about 2 pounds), such as sole, flounder, or perch

1 small onion, minced

2 tablespoons butter or margarine

1 tablespoon seasoned bread crumbs

Toasted almonds for topping

In a large bowl, beat the eggs, water, and hot pepper sauce. Add the fish fillets and let marinate in the refrigerator for 10 to 15 minutes. Meanwhile, in a large skillet, sauté the onion in the butter over medium heat. When the onion is just softened, sprinkle the bread crumbs over the bottom of the skillet. Remove the fillets from the egg mixture, reserving mixture, and lay them on top of the crumbs. Cook for 4 to 5 minutes. Turn the fillets over, spoon the reserved egg mixture over them, and cook for 3 to 4 minutes more. Reduce the heat to low, cover, and cook for 1 to 2 minutes more. The egg coating should be puffy and light golden brown. Sprinkle fish with toasted almonds and serve.

NOTE: For a different taste, you can use shallots instead of onions or add a teaspoon of chopped green bell pepper to the onions. Or sprinkle on some Parmesan cheese instead of the almonds. Or sprinkle on some finely chopped fresh dill or basil. Get the picture? Do your own thing.

Orange-Broiled Swordfish

6 servings

Looking for something different to do with fish? Here it is, and any fish steak—such as tuna, shark, halibut, or salmon—can be used. During our heavy orange season, it's nice to garnish this with seedless orange slices—it'll remind us of sunny California and Florida.

3 cups barbecue sauce

1 teaspoon grated orange rind

1 teaspoon ground ginger or ½ teaspoon grated fresh ginger

2 tablespoons soy sauce

6 6-ounce swordfish steaks

Peanut oil

Preheat broiler. Combine the barbecue sauce, orange rind, ginger, and soy sauce in a medium-sized saucepan and heat to a simmer. Remove from heat. Brush the swordfish steaks on both sides with the oil and place on a rack in a baking pan. Brush steaks generously on both sides with sauce, reserving excess for basting. Cover and refrigerate for at least an hour. Broil swordfish for 3 to 4 minutes on each side, basting often with sauce, until cooked through.

Super Shrimp Casserole

4 servings

Who doesn't like shrimp, mushrooms, and cheese? Here's a way to combine all these favorite ingredients into one easy, super dish.

- 1 pound cooked shrimp, peeled and deveined
- Salt and pepper to taste
- ½ pound fresh mushrooms, sliced
- 3 tablespoons butter or margarine plus 4 tablespoons softened butter or margarine
- 1 tablespoon all-purpose flour
- 1 cup (8 ounces) sour cream
- 1 teaspoon soy sauce
- ¼ cup grated Parmesan cheese
- 1 teaspoon paprika

Preheat oven to 400°F. Arrange the shrimp in a single layer in a greased shallow baking dish. Sprinkle with salt and pepper. In a medium-sized skillet, sauté the mushrooms in 3 tablespoons butter until lightly browned. Transfer them to a medium-sized bowl and toss with the flour. Stir in the sour cream, the 4 tablespoons softened butter, soy sauce, and salt and pepper to taste. Pour mushroom sauce over the shrimp; sprinkle with the Parmesan cheese and paprika. Bake for 10 to 12 minutes or until bubbly.

NOTE: I like to serve the shrimp over rice or noodles.

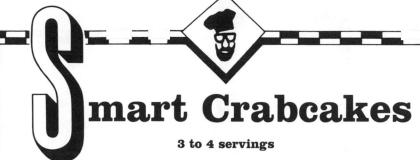

Smart Crabcakes

3 to 4 servings

Nothing tastes more like summer than crabcakes. The only problem is the price of the crab. Well, here are a few little twists that will let us enjoy crabcakes for a lot less money (easier, too!).

½ **pound crabmeat, broken up**

½ **pound imitation crabmeat, broken up**

2 **tablespoons mayonnaise**

1 **teaspoon finely chopped green bell pepper**

1 **teaspoon dried parsley flakes**

1 **teaspoon prepared mustard**

1 **teaspoon seafood seasoning (optional)**

¼ **teaspoon salt**

¼ **teaspoon pepper**

1 **egg, beaten**

3 **slices white bread with crusts, crumbled**

Butter or margarine for browning

In a large bowl, combine all ingredients except the butter. Mix well and form into 6 or 8 patties. Melt butter in a large frying pan and cook patties over medium-high heat until browned on both sides.

NOTE: You also could use poached fish instead of the crabmeat or use half imitation crabmeat and half fish, or just all imitation crab.

Tuna Niçoise

about 8 servings

An even-better-than-with-mayonnaise tuna salad is nice once in a while—it's Mediterranean-fancy but good old American-easy.

- 4 cans (6½ ounces each) tuna, drained
- ½ cup bottled Italian dressing
- 1 can (2 ounces) anchovies, drained
- ¼ cup chopped red onion
- ½ cup chopped pitted black olives
- ½ red bell pepper, chopped

In a blender or food processor, process the tuna, Italian dressing, and anchovies until smooth, stopping occasionally to scrape down sides of container. Pour mixture into a medium-sized bowl, and stir in the chopped onion, olives, and red pepper.

NOTE: This is great served with fresh salad vegetables.

Tuna Anchovy Spread

about 1½ cups

For entertaining or just for enjoying yourself, here's an easy way to have that great tuna-anchovy taste in a spread form.

4 ounces cream cheese, softened

8 tablespoons (1 stick) unsalted butter, softened

1 can (6½ ounces) solid white tuna, drained

¾ to 1 teaspoon anchovy paste (to taste)

Salt and white pepper to taste

In a medium-sized bowl, mix all ingredients together until well combined.

NOTE: Spread on party rye bread slices and serve.

Halibut Wealthy-Style

4 servings

This takes halibut steaks (or swordfish steaks or fresh tuna steaks) and brings them up to the fancy company level. And you can use oregano or rosemary or cumin or cayenne pepper instead of dill—a different one each time for some extra novelty. It makes us look so kitchen-creative.

4 halibut steaks (approximately 8 ounces each)

MARINADE

½ cup bottled French dressing

2 tablespoons lemon *or* lime juice

TOPPING

1 cup canned French-fried onion rings, crushed

½ cup grated Parmesan cheese

¼ teaspoon dried dillweed

Chopped fresh parsley for garnish (optional)

Lemon or lime wedges for garnish (optional)

In a small bowl, mix the marinade ingredients. Put the halibut steaks in a shallow pan and pour the marinade over them; let marinate in the refrigerator for 20 to 30 minutes, basting steaks occasionally with the marinade. Preheat oven to 350°F. In a small bowl, mix together all the topping ingredients. Remove the halibut from the marinade and place in a well-greased 9"x13" glass baking dish. Sprinkle the topping mixture over the fish. Bake for 20 to

30 minutes (depending on the thickness of the fish), until the flesh flakes easily when tested with a fork. Garnish with chopped parsley and lemon or lime wedges if desired.

Smart Shrimp Salad

3 to 4 servings

Make this when you're tired of serving shrimp the way everybody does—when you want something a little different for a change, but still easy. Try a dash of hot pepper sauce or a pinch of garlic powder or oregano. Put sliced cucumbers around the serving platter. Do your own thing—it'll look and taste great.

- 1 pound cooked shrimp, peeled and deveined
- ½ pound Jarlsberg cheese, cut into ½-inch cubes
- ⅔ cup mayonnaise
- 1 tablespoon fresh lemon juice
- 1 tablespoon honey
- ¼ cup chopped scallions
- 2 teaspoons curry powder

In a large bowl, mix the shrimp and cheese. In a small bowl, combine the mayonnaise, lemon juice, honey, scallions, and curry powder; mix well. Stir the mayonnaise mixture into the shrimp-cheese mixture until well mixed. Serve immediately or refrigerate until ready to serve.

NOTE: Tiny salad shrimp or even broken pieces will work fine. Use whatever's on sale!

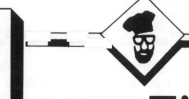

Lemon Fillets

2 servings

This is about as easy as fish can be, but it tastes gourmet-fussed. I like to dab the fish with a touch of mustard or a sprinkle of garlic powder and sometimes some Cajun or Tex-Mex seasoning, but you don't have to.

4 tablespoons (¼ cup) butter or margarine

½ teaspoon dried dillweed

½ teaspoon dried thyme

1 scallion, thinly sliced

1 tablespoon lemon juice

1 pound fish fillets

Lemon slices for garnish

In a large skillet, melt the butter and stir in the dillweed, thyme, scallion, and lemon juice. Add the fish fillets and cook for 4 to 5 minutes, or until fish flakes easily when tested with a fork. Put fish on a serving platter and pour butter sauce from skillet over the fillets. Garnish with lemon slices.

NOTE: Any kind of fish fillets will work—try haddock, bluefish, flounder, or grouper.

S eafood Salad

3 to 4 servings

The perfect easy salad to serve any lunch time or for a summer dinner. Your family will think you fussed (and so will your company)—especially when it's served on a bed of dark green lettuce like romaine or escarole or even iceberg!

¾ **pound imitation crabmeat, chunked or flaked**

⅓ **cup sharp Cheddar cheese, cut into cubes**

1 **small can (4.2 ounces) pitted ripe olives, coarsely chopped**

2 **scallions, thinly sliced**

1 **to 2 ribs celery, diced**

½ **teaspoon seafood seasoning**

Mayonnaise to moisten

Chopped fresh parsley for garnish

Combine the crabmeat, cheese, olives, scallions, celery, and seafood seasoning in a medium-sized bowl. Add mayonnaise to moisten. Chill for 1 to 2 hours. Top with chopped parsley and serve.

Burgers on the Shelf

4 servings

Getting bored with the same old hamburger? Well, not anymore. Hooray! Here's a salmon burger that's like a hamburger—but it's a nice change.

EASIEST DILL SAUCE

- 1 cup (8 ounces) sour cream
- ½ cup mayonnaise
- 1 teaspoon dried dillweed
- 2 teaspoons lemon juice
- 1 tablespoon sweet pickle relish

- 1 can (15½ ounces) salmon (pink, chum, or red), drained, flaked, and boned

- 1 cup seasoned bread crumbs
- 4 eggs, beaten
- ⅓ cup finely chopped onion
- 1 tablespoon chopped fresh parsley
- ⅛ teaspoon black pepper
- Salt to taste (optional)
- 2 tablespoons vegetable oil (for pan frying only)

In a small bowl, mix all the sauce ingredients together. In a large bowl, mix together all the remaining ingredients except the oil. Shape mixture into 4 burger-sized patties.

Outdoor Grill Method:

Place the patties in a greased hinged grill basket and grill them over a medium fire on the barbecue, turning once, until golden brown. Spoon the Easiest Dill Sauce over patties and serve.

Pan-Fried Method:

In a large skillet, heat the oil over medium heat. Fry the patties, turning once, until golden brown. Spoon the sauce over the patties before serving.

Golden Fish Fillets

4 servings

They'll never believe the coating is potato flakes—that's right, potato flakes!

1 egg

2 tablespoons prepared mustard

½ teaspoon salt

Instant mashed potato flakes to coat

1½ to 2 pounds white-fleshed fish fillets, such as sole, flounder, or perch

Vegetable oil or solid vegetable shortening

Lightly beat together the egg, mustard, and salt in a shallow dish. Put the potato flakes in another shallow dish. Dip the fish fillets in egg mixture; then roll in potato flakes to coat. Heat oil in a large skillet. Fry fish for 3 to 4 minutes on each side, until it is golden brown and flakes easily with a fork.

Southern-Style Fish Chili

4 to 6 servings

Everyone has a chili recipe—but not like this one, they don't! And with everybody into fish 'cause it's lighter, they'll reach for seconds . . . and maybe for thirds and fourths!

- 2 pounds white-fleshed fish fillets (such as cod, haddock, or sole), thawed if frozen, cut into 1-inch pieces
- 1 large onion, sliced
- 1 cup diced green bell pepper
- 1 garlic clove, minced
- 2 tablespoons butter or vegetable oil
- 1½ teaspoons salt
- 1½ teaspoons chili powder
- ½ teaspoon oregano
- ¼ teaspoon pepper
- 1 can (1 pound) red kidney beans, undrained
- 1 can (14.5 ounces) whole tomatoes, undrained
- 1 can (6 ounces) tomato paste
- Chopped fresh parsley for garnish

In a 5-quart Dutch oven, sauté the onion, green pepper, and garlic in butter until onion is tender; do not let it brown. Stir in the salt, chili powder, oregano, and pepper. Add the kidney beans, tomatoes, and tomato paste. Heat until simmering, stirring occasionally. Add the fish, cover, and reduce heat. Simmer gently for 8 to 10 minutes or until fish flakes easily with a fork. Garnish with chopped fresh parsley.

POTATOES AND RICE

P otatoes and rice, the two main "go-alongs." They're staples, they're fillers, they're many people's favorite part of the meal, and they're also very versatile. Everybody adds to, adapts, seasons in different ways, and otherwise experiments with them. Potatoes are enjoyed every way from mashed to barbecue grilled, and rice is popular whether it's just plain boiled or all fancied up.

If you're looking for the down-home recipes, they're in here. If you're looking for the fancies, they're in here too. But they're all in here as easy and tasty. Actually, the down-homes and the fancies are the same ones! It just depends on how you serve them.

TIDBIT: So many people think that they must buy baking potatoes for baked potatoes—Unh-uh! Any potatoes can be baked. Scrub them under cold running water, pat them dry, prick them with a fork, and bake; the skin might not be as thick as you're used to, but they'll still taste great. In order for the potatoes all to be done at the same time, though, it's always smart to keep them approximately the same size.

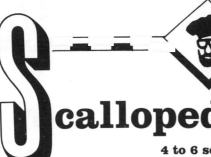

Scalloped Potatoes

4 to 6 servings

Scalloped? Au gratin? Creamed? Whatever you call them, everyone will say **OOH it's so GOOD!!**™

- ½ cup milk
- 1 teaspoon Italian seasoning
- ½ teaspoon salt
- 1 teaspoon onion powder
- ¼ teaspoon white pepper

- 3 medium-sized boiling potatoes, peeled and cut into ¼-inch-thick slices
- 2 tablespoons butter or margarine
- ½ cup (2 ounces) grated Cheddar cheese
- 2 tablespoons grated Parmesan cheese
- Paprika

Preheat oven to 350°F. Grease a 2-quart casserole dish. Combine the milk, Italian seasoning, salt, onion powder, and pepper in a small bowl. Arrange potato slices in casserole dish. Pour milk mixture over potatoes. Dot with butter. Cover and bake for 1 hour or until potatoes are tender. Remove cover and sprinkle cheeses and paprika over potatoes. Bake, uncovered, for 8 to 10 minutes longer, until cheeses are melted. Serve hot.

NOTE: If you feel like going a little heavier on the seasonings, go ahead! It'll make it fuller tasting. In fact, I like it better that way.

Parmesan Potato Sticks

5 to 6 servings

Here's a dandy change from everyday French fries. They're tender on the inside and cheese-tasting crispy on the outside. If you want them a little browner and crispier, a little longer in the oven will do it.

½ cup fine dry bread crumbs

½ cup grated Parmesan cheese

⅛ teaspoon garlic powder

½ teaspoon salt

⅛ teaspoon pepper

2 pounds baking potatoes

8 tablespoons (1 stick) butter or margarine, melted

Preheat oven to 400°F. In a small bowl, mix together the bread crumbs, Parmesan cheese, garlic powder, salt, and pepper; set aside. Peel the potatoes and cut lengthwise into quarters; cut each quarter lengthwise into 3 strips. Dip each strip in the melted butter, then in the Parmesan mixture, making sure potatoes are well coated. Place in a single layer in a large baking dish (or dishes) greased with nonstick vegetable spray. Pour any remaining melted butter over potatoes. Bake for 30 to 35 minutes, until potatoes are tender, turning them once or twice.

Potato-Cheese Casserole

6 to 8 servings

If you wanna get this ready beforehand, you can bake it up to a day ahead and just reheat it in the microwave. A nice go-along dish.

- 4 medium-sized baking potatoes
- 2 cans (10¾ ounces each) condensed cream of mushroom soup
- 1½ cups milk
- 2 medium-sized onions, thinly sliced
- 2 cups (8 ounces) shredded sharp Cheddar cheese
- Salt and pepper to taste
- Paprika

Preheat oven to 300°F. Put the potatoes in a large pot, add enough salted water to cover, and bring to a boil; boil gently for 25 to 30 minutes, or until tender. Let potatoes cool, peel them, and cut into ¼-inch-thick slices. In a medium-sized bowl, combine the soup and milk, stirring well. Arrange half the potatoes in the bottom of a greased 2-quart casserole; arrange half the sliced onions on top, and sprinkle half the Cheddar cheese over them. Add salt and pepper to taste. Pour half the soup mixture over the potatoes. Repeat layers and pour remaining soup mixture over top; sprinkle with paprika. Bake for 45 to 50 minutes or until bubbly.

The Other Baked Potatoes

4 servings

Try adding smoked turkey instead of the bacon, or maybe add some diced smoked cheese. My favorite way is to sprinkle on some chili powder or a few tablespoons of tomato sauce. They'll probably accuse you of stealing some fancy restaurant's recipe, but so what! You'll know the truth.

4 or 5 medium-sized potatoes, peeled and diced

1 medium-sized onion, chopped

3 slices cooked bacon, chopped

¼ cup white vinegar

¼ cup light molasses

¼ cup firmly packed brown sugar

1 teaspoon dry mustard

1 teaspoon salt

Preheat oven to 400°F. Combine all ingredients in a large bowl and toss gently to mix. Put into a greased 2-quart casserole dish. Bake, covered, for about 1 hour or until potatoes are tender.

NOTE: You can cook the potatoes uncovered for an additional 10 minutes to give them a nice brown crust.

Potato Pudding

4 to 6 servings

Make it your family's very, very own by adding some garlic or onion powder, or some chopped scallions or parsley. It's guaranteed that this will become one of your favorites.

- 4 medium-sized potatoes, peeled
- 1 cup grated Parmesan cheese
- 2 eggs
- 4 tablespoons (¼ cup) butter or margarine
- 1 cup milk
- ¼ teaspoon salt
- ⅛ teaspoon pepper

Preheat oven to 400°F. Put the potatoes in a large pot, add enough water to cover, and boil for 25 to 30 minutes, until tender. Drain potatoes and mash while still warm. Add the remaining ingredients to the potatoes and mix well. Put mixture in a well-greased 1½-quart baking dish and bake for 30 to 40 minutes, or until top of pudding is golden brown.

Potato Pancakes

5 to 6 large pancakes

Everybody makes potato pancakes a little bit differently. Here's my own favorite way, and remember, they're not just for holiday time.

2 cups (about 1½ pounds or 2 to 3 large) peeled baking potatoes

½ cup finely chopped onion

1 egg, beaten

½ cup all-purpose flour

1 teaspoon baking powder

Salt and white pepper to taste

Vegetable oil for frying

Coarsely grate the potatoes and put them and the onion in a strainer. Press down on them with the back of a large spoon to extract excess moisture. (If they're still watery, wrap them in a clean dishtowel and squeeze to extract moisture.) In a large bowl, combine the potatoes, onion, and egg; mix well. Gradually add the flour and baking powder, mixing well, and season with salt and pepper. Heat ¼ inch oil in a large heavy skillet over medium to medium-high heat. Using about ¼ cup of batter for each pancake, add batter to the hot oil, being careful not to crowd pan. Fry, turning once, until pancakes are golden on both sides. (If you like them crisper, fry until they're flecked with brown.) Drain on paper towels and serve hot.

NOTE: It's preferable to use baking potatoes in this recipe because they have less moisture. Sometimes I like to use bread crumbs or matzo meal (or a combination) instead of flour.

Striped Spuds

4 to 6 servings

When you have the grill going, why not grill your potatoes? That's right—potatoes! We do meats, poultry, and even fish on the grill, so why not potatoes, too?!

4 large baking potatoes

BASTING SAUCE
4 tablespoons (¼ cup) butter or margarine, melted

2 tablespoons spicy mustard

1 teaspoon sugar

½ teaspoon seasoned salt

½ teaspoon Italian seasoning

Put the potatoes in a large pot, add enough salted water to cover, and boil until just tender, 20 to 25 minutes. Meanwhile, mix together all the basting sauce ingredients. Drain potatoes, let cool, and peel if desired. Cut potatoes into ¾-inch-thick slices. Brush generously with sauce. Grill over hot coals, turning once, until deep golden brown on both sides.

NOTE: To make turning the potatoes a little easier, I like to put them in a greased hinged grill basket.

Picnic Potato Salad

about 10 servings

Everyone has a recipe for potato salad. But here's one that gives you potato salad and vegetable salad all in one.

DRESSING

- 1 cup mayonnaise
- 2 tablespoons Dijon mustard
- ¼ cup white wine vinegar
- ¼ cup vegetable oil
- ½ teaspoon salt
- ⅛ teaspoon pepper

- 3 pounds boiling potatoes, cooked, peeled, and cut into ½-inch cubes
- ½ cup chopped fresh parsley

- ½ cup thinly sliced red onion
- ½ cup thinly sliced celery
- 1 medium cucumber, peeled, seeded, and chopped
- 3 hard-cooked eggs, peeled and quartered lengthwise, for garnish (optional)

  Fresh chopped parsley for garnish (optional)

In a small bowl, stir together all the dressing ingredients. In a large bowl, combine the potatoes, ½ cup parsley, red onion, celery, and cucumber. Pour dressing over vegetables and toss gently to coat. Cover and refrigerate for several hours or overnight. Toss gently before serving and garnish with eggs and parsley, if desired.

Stuffed Sweet Potatoes

4 servings

Tired of the same old potatoes? Well, here's a new easy twist on an old standby that turns whatever you serve them with into a more special dish. Yams do that all the time—they've got a holiday touch to them.

- **4 medium-sized sweet potatoes or yams**
  Vegetable oil
- **½ cup firmly packed brown sugar**
- **½ cup evaporated milk**
- **⅓ cup orange juice**

- **¼ teaspoon cinnamon**
  Pinch of salt
- **1 tablespoon fresh or 1 teaspoon dried grated orange rind**
- **1 cup flaked coconut (optional)**

Preheat oven to 375°F. Scrub the potatoes thoroughly and rub with oil. Put in a shallow baking pan, prick top of each with a fork, and bake for 1 hour, or until tender. Remove from oven, and lower oven temperature to 350°F. Let potatoes cool, and cut a slice from the top of each one. Carefully scoop out pulp, leaving shells intact. In a large bowl, combine the potato pulp, sugar, milk, orange juice, cinnamon, and salt; beat with an electric mixer until smooth. Stir in the orange rind and ½ cup coconut. Spoon potato mixture back into shells. Sprinkle with remaining ½ cup coconut. Bake for 20 minutes or until heated through.

Half-Baked Sweet Potatoes with Lemon Butter Sauce

4 servings

There are so many delicious ways to make sweet potatoes— and here's another one. See how few ingredients? Well, that's how easy it is—so when you don't wanna fool around with getting a lot of items together but you still want them to be more than just everyday, try these.

- **4 medium-sized sweet potatoes**
- **8 tablespoons (1 stick) butter or margarine**
- **3 tablespoons lemon juice**
- **2 tablespoons finely chopped fresh parsley**
- **¼ teaspoon salt**

Preheat oven to 400°F. Scrub the sweet potatoes and pat dry. Cut potatoes in half lengthwise; prick skins with a fork. Place cut-side down in a greased shallow baking pan. Bake for 35 to 40 minutes or until tender. Meanwhile, melt the butter in a small saucepan; stir in the lemon juice, parsley, and salt. Serve with the potatoes.

Caramel-Glazed Sweet Potatoes

4 servings

Enjoy holiday-style potatoes any time. These are easy and delicious. They're so easy because the bottled butterscotch topping does so much of the home-style flavoring for us.

2 cups sweet potatoes (about 2 large potatoes), cooked, peeled, and cut into 1-inch chunks

½ teaspoon salt

⅓ cup butterscotch dessert topping

Preheat oven to 350°F. Put the sweet potato chunks in an ungreased 8-inch square baking dish; season with the salt. Spoon butterscotch topping over potatoes. Bake, uncovered, for 25 to 30 minutes or until tender, basting occasionally with sauce that accumulates in pan.

Dill New Potato Salad

about 12 servings

This works nicely with the little new potatoes (red or white). I like to leave the skins on the red potatoes for color and texture. Serve this warm or cold.

5 pounds new potatoes	¾ cup chopped scallions
1 cup (8 ounces) sour cream	2 teaspoons chopped garlic
3 tablespoons dried dillweed	Dash Worcestershire sauce
½ teaspoon salt	Dash hot pepper sauce
½ teaspoon pepper	

Put potatoes in a large pot, add enough water to cover, and boil for 18 to 20 minutes, or until tender. Drain, let cool slightly, and cut into quarters. In a large bowl, combine all remaining ingredients and mix well. Add the potatoes, toss gently to coat, and serve immediately, or refrigerate until chilled.

NOTE: Garnish with fresh dill and sliced scallions, if desired.

Really Rich Rice

4 to 6 servings

Wow! A side dish that's French-simple, French-fancy! It's rice with a richer taste. Even those people who don't usually eat rice will eat rice this way. Making it ahead of time and rewarming it in the oven or microwave can make it easier for us.

1 **large onion, diced**

2 **tablespoons butter or margarine**

2 **cups cooked white rice**

2 **eggs, beaten**

1 **cup milk**

1 **cup (4 ounces) shredded Swiss cheese**

¼ **teaspoon salt**

Pepper to taste

Chopped fresh parsley for garnish

Paprika for garnish

Preheat oven to 375° F. In a large skillet, sauté the onion in the butter for 5 to 7 minutes or until golden. Stir in the remaining ingredients, mixing well, and turn into a greased 1½-quart baking dish. Bake for 20 to 25 minutes until set. Sprinkle with chopped parsley and paprika to garnish.

Easy Spanish Rice

4 servings

A rice dish as a main course—hearty and healthy, too!

2 tablespoons vegetable oil	1 teaspoon seasoned salt
1 pound lean ground beef	½ teaspoon ground cumin
1 cup finely chopped onion	½ teaspoon black pepper
1 cup finely chopped green bell pepper	1 can (8 ounces) tomato sauce
1 cup long-grain white rice	1 can (14½ ounces) whole tomatoes, drained and coarsely chopped (optional)
2 teaspoons chili powder	
1½ cups water	

In a large skillet, heat the oil over medium heat. Add the beef, onion, and green pepper, and cook, stirring, until meat has lost its pink color. Drain off grease. Stir in remaining ingredients; reduce heat, cover, and simmer for 20 minutes or until rice is tender.

NOTE: Sometimes I use ground turkey or veal instead of the beef.

Rice Nut Dressing

8 to 10 servings

Want a special dressing for the holidays? It doesn't have to be served instead of the traditional favorite bread dressing. Why not surprise and delight your family by putting this one on the table, too?!

1½ cups finely chopped onion

1½ cups finely chopped celery

2 tablespoons butter or margarine

6 cups cooked white rice (cooked in chicken broth)

1 cup raisins

⅔ cup chopped walnuts

¼ cup honey

2 tablespoons lemon juice

1½ teaspoons salt

½ teaspoon ground cinnamon

½ teaspoon pepper

Preheat oven to 350°F. In a large skillet, sauté the onion and celery in butter until crisp-tender. Stir in remaining ingredients and mix well. Turn into a greased 2-quart casserole. Cover and bake for 30 to 35 minutes or until heated through.

NOTE: Sometimes I use chopped pecans instead of the walnuts and I might even add a few sliced mushrooms.

arden Rice Salad

6 to 8 servings

Here's a change from potato and macaroni salads: a rice and vegetable salad. Doesn't that fit today's smart eating style? And it's fun 'cause you can try substituting red peppers for green peppers or onions for scallions, or be adventurous and add some fresh parsley or chopped cucumber, or try brown rice for a change of pace. It'll all work and it'll always be a winner.

4 cups cooked white rice

1 package (10 ounces) frozen peas, thawed

½ cup diced green bell pepper

½ cup finely diced celery

¼ cup mayonnaise

2 tablespoons finely chopped scallions

2 tablespoons finely chopped radishes

1 garlic clove, minced

¼ teaspoon salt

2 tablespoons honey

1 teaspoon curry powder

½ teaspoon ground nutmeg

Combine all ingredients in a medium-sized serving bowl. Refrigerate for 3 to 4 hours until well chilled, and serve.

PASTA

Remember how Momma used to say, "Shouldn't eat too much pasta, it's fattening, not good for you"? Well, ha, ha, ha! It's turned out to be one of the big energy foods. All the "health" people are promoting it as the "wonder food." And pasta is simple to make—you just boil it. It goes perfectly with everything you mix into it, from bottled sauces (or a simple, "doctored" bottled sauce that tastes homemade garden fresh) to still simple but exotic "gourmet-sounding" sauces. Serve it with meat or fish, as a side dish, or as a main dish—you name it, and it's still simple. There's that word again: *simple.* I love it.

Have fun with these recipes. And remember, pasta is popular to start with, so you've got a head start on getting those smiles.

Pasta and Spinach

4 main-course servings

Kind of like a lasagna pudding—you know, that great taste without all the work. And you can vary it, too. Wanna add sausage? How about fennel seed or a shake of oregano or garlic powder? Make it ahead if that's easier, 'cause it gets better and better.

- 1 pound short tubular pasta, such as ziti or rigatoni

- 2 tablespoons grated Parmesan cheese

SAUCE
- ⅔ cup grated Parmesan cheese

- 2 packages (10 ounces each) frozen chopped spinach, thawed and drained well

- 1 pound (16 ounces) ricotta cheese

- 3 eggs, beaten

- ⅓ cup chopped fresh parsley

- 2 teaspoons salt (or to taste)

- 2 teaspoons pepper

- 1 quart (32 ounces) spaghetti sauce

Preheat oven to 375°F. In a large pot of boiling water, cook pasta for 1 to 2 minutes less than the time indicated on the package, or until just barely tender. Meanwhile, in a large bowl, combine the ⅔ cup Parmesan cheese and all the other sauce ingredients; mix well. Drain the pasta, toss it with the sauce, and turn it into a greased 9"x13" baking dish. Sprinkle the 2 tablespoons Parmesan over top and bake for 25 to 30 minutes until bubbly and lightly browned on top.

Shrimp and Pasta Toss

6 to 8 appetizer servings

If you want to add a little oregano or basil, or maybe some chili powder for a Tex-Mex taste, go for it. Every time you make this you can have a new taste that fits whatever else you're serving.

- 1 pound rotini or shell-shaped pasta
- ¾ cup mild barbecue sauce
- 1 cup mayonnaise
- ½ cup grated Parmesan cheese
- ¼ cup red wine vinegar
- ¾ pound cooked shrimp, peeled and deveined
- 1½ cups diced celery
- ½ cup diced onion
- Chopped fresh parsley for garnish (optional)

In a large pot of boiling salted water, cook pasta just until tender. Meanwhile, in a medium-sized bowl, combine the barbecue sauce, mayonnaise, cheese, and vinegar. Drain the pasta, rinse under cold water and drain, and put into a large bowl. Add the shrimp, celery, and onion and toss gently. Add the barbecue sauce mixture and toss again to mix. Cover and refrigerate until chilled. Garnish with chopped fresh parsley, if desired.

Spaghetti Bolognese

4 main-course servings

A shortcut spaghetti sauce for when you're in a hurry. You can add the bouillon cube for richness, or use ground pork or veal instead of beef. Give it your own special touch!

1 pound ground beef

1 cup shredded carrots

⅔ cup chopped onion

1 garlic clove, crushed

1 teaspoon dried basil leaves, crushed

1 teaspoon dried oregano, crushed

1 beef bouillon cube (optional)

1 teaspoon sugar

½ teaspoon Italian seasoning

2 cans (15 ounces each) tomato sauce

1 pound spaghetti

In a large skillet, brown the beef over medium-high heat. Drain off fat. Add the carrots, onion, and garlic. Cook, stirring, for about 5 minutes or until onion is tender. Add all the remaining ingredients except the spaghetti. Cover, reduce heat, and simmer for 18 to 20 minutes, stirring occasionally. Meanwhile, in a large pot of boiling salted water, cook the spaghetti just until tender. Drain, put into a serving bowl, and pour the sauce over.

Turkey Lasagna

6 to 8 main-course servings

Here's a new twist on an old, down-home Italian classic. It's using the lighter ground turkey that does the "new" part.

1 cup (4 ounces) shredded mozzarella cheese

1 cup (8 ounces) ricotta cheese

¼ cup grated Parmesan cheese

1 pound ground turkey

2 tablespoons vegetable oil

1 garlic clove, crushed

1 can (4 ounces) mushroom pieces and stems, undrained

1 jar (15½ ounces) spaghetti sauce

10 strips lasagna

4 to 5 slices mozzarella cheese for topping

Preheat oven to 350°F. In a small bowl, combine the shredded mozzarella cheese, the ricotta cheese, and the Parmesan cheese; set aside. In a large skillet, brown the ground turkey in the oil. Add the crushed garlic, mushrooms, and spaghetti sauce. Bring to a boil, reduce heat, and simmer. Meanwhile, in a large pot of boiling salted water, cook the lasagna just until tender; drain. Rinse and pat dry. Pour about one third of the meat sauce over the bottom of a greased 9"x13" baking dish, add a layer of lasagna strips, and pour another third of the meat sauce over. Carefully spread half the cheese mixture over sauce. Add another layer of strips, the remaining meat sauce, and the remainder of the cheese mixture. Top with mozzarella slices. Bake for 25 to 30 minutes until golden brown. Let set for 15 minutes before cutting into servings.

NOTE: If you wanna give this a hint of sausage flavor, crush 1 teaspoon fennel seed and add it to the sauce. A one-pound box of lasagna contains about 20 strips.

Fettuccine Alfredo

2 main-course servings, 4 appetizer servings

Sound fancy and difficult? Well, it's really easy and fast. Just do your own thing—try sprinkling on either nutmeg or fresh parsley or garlic.

- 8 ounces fettuccine, linguine, or medium egg noodles
- 4 tablespoons (¼ cup) butter, melted
- ¼ cup grated Parmesan cheese
- 2 tablespoons half-and-half
- ¼ teaspoon salt
- ¼ teaspoon pepper

In a large pot of boiling water, cook pasta just until tender; drain. In a heated serving dish, combine all the remaining ingredients. Add the hot drained pasta and carefully toss to coat well.

NOTE: If desired, sprinkle pasta with freshly ground pepper and additional Parmesan cheese.

Lasagna Roll-Ups

6 to 7 main-course servings

Here's a new twist on an old favorite. Add a little more parsley or some browned sausage for some variety.

- 15 strips lasagna
- 1 quart (32 ounces) spaghetti sauce
- 1 cup (4 ounces) shredded mozzarella cheese

FILLING
- 2 pounds (32 ounces) ricotta cheese

- 1 cup (4 ounces) shredded mozzarella cheese
- ⅓ cup grated Parmesan cheese
- 3 eggs, beaten
- 1 tablespoon chopped fresh parsley
- 1 teaspoon salt

Preheat oven to 375°F. In a large pot of boiling water, cook lasagna until just barely tender. Meanwhile, in a large bowl, mix all the filling ingredients together. Pour half the spaghetti sauce over the bottom of a 9"x13" baking dish coated with a nonstick vegetable spray. Drain the lasagna, rinse, and pat dry. Lay the strips out flat and spread the filling evenly over each strip. Roll the strips up and arrange them in the baking dish seam-side down. Pour remaining sauce over, and top with the mozzarella cheese. Bake for 35 to 40 minutes until bubbly and golden brown. Let set for about 12 to 15 minutes before serving.

NOTE: A one-pound box of lasagna contains about 20 strips.

American Pasta Salad

6 to 8 side-dish servings

This is ready to eat right away, but if you can store it covered in the refrigerator overnight—wait 'til you taste it then! Makes a great snack, lunch, or dinner—it's just fine anytime.

1 pound pasta (shells or twists)

2 cups mayonnaise

¼ cup grated Parmesan cheese

¼ cup red wine vinegar

1 teaspoon dried oregano

1 teaspoon dried thyme

½ teaspoon salt

½ teaspoon pepper

½ teaspoon garlic powder

6 hard-boiled eggs, peeled and chopped

1 cup diced mozzarella cheese

1 red bell pepper, coarsely chopped

4 or 5 scallions, finely chopped

In a large pot of boiling water, cook pasta until tender. Meanwhile, in a large bowl, blend the mayonnaise, Parmesan cheese, vinegar, oregano, thyme, salt, pepper, and garlic powder. Drain and rinse pasta and add to the mayonnaise mixture; mix well. Add the chopped eggs, mozzarella cheese, red pepper, and scallions. Mix just until combined. Serve immediately, or cover and chill for several hours or overnight to blend flavors.

NOTE: Add some diced salami or pepperoni and the salad becomes a whole meal in itself. For flavor variations, add ½ teaspoon dillweed or basil.

Special Macaroni and Cheese

4 main-course servings

This popular standard just became a little more special, and it's still just as easy. Everybody's gonna ask for this recipe—you'll see!

- 1 pound elbow macaroni
- 2 tablespoons vegetable oil
- ½ pound fresh mushrooms, sliced
- 1 medium onion, finely chopped
- 1 cup sliced celery
- 1 can (10¾ ounces) condensed cream of mushroom soup
- 3 cups (12 ounces) grated sharp Cheddar cheese

Preheat oven to 350°F. In a large pot of boiling salted water, cook macaroni just until tender. Meanwhile, in a medium-sized skillet heat oil; sauté the mushrooms, onion, and celery until tender. Drain the macaroni (*do not rinse*). Mix the mushroom soup, Cheddar cheese, sautéed mushroom mixture, and the macaroni in a large bowl. Pour into a 9"x13" glass baking dish greased with non-stick vegetable spray. Bake for 35 to 40 minutes until lightly browned.

NOTE: You might want to put this dish together a day ahead, cover it, and refrigerate; then bake it when needed. If you'd like to vary it a little, you might add some chopped green bell pepper to the other sautéed vegetables, a minced garlic clove or a sprinkle of garlic powder, and/or a teaspoon of dillweed, thyme, or tarragon. Also, if you use mild Cheddar cheese instead of sharp, you might want to add ½ teaspoon salt.

acaroni Holiday

2 main-course servings

Want something that whips up in a hurry? This makes a great meal or a great side dish, from hot dog-comfortable to ham-fancy. (You can leave out the meat if you want.)

8 ounces elbow macaroni

1 can (10¾ ounces) condensed cream of mushroom *or* celery soup

1 teaspoon dry mustard

1 cup milk

1 cup (4 ounces) grated Cheddar cheese

1½ cups luncheon meat, cut into ½-inch cubes (about ½ pound)

¼ cup chopped green bell pepper

Black pepper to taste

Preheat oven to 325°F. In a large pot of boiling salted water, cook macaroni just until tender. Meanwhile, in a medium-sized saucepan, combine the soup, mustard, milk, and cheese. Bring to a simmer, stirring occasionally, and cook just until cheese is melted. Drain the macaroni and put into a large bowl. Add the soup mixture, luncheon meat, green pepper, and black pepper. Pour into a 1½-quart greased casserole dish. Bake for 25 to 30 minutes, until bubbly and lightly browned.

NOTE: I like to slice additional luncheon meat into ½-inch strips and arrange on top of casserole before baking. Sometimes I even use hot dogs or ham instead of the luncheon meat.

acaroni Everything

4 main-course servings

Wanna raise some eyebrows? Well, this anything-you-want-to-add-to-it pasta dish may be just the ticket!

1 pound macaroni (any type)	1 can (14½ ounces) whole tomatoes, drained
½ cup grated Parmesan cheese	1 teaspoon salt
¼ cup olive oil	¼ teaspoon pepper

In a large pot of boiling water, cook the macaroni until tender; drain and put into a large bowl. Add ¼ cup of the Parmesan cheese, the olive oil, tomatoes, salt, and pepper; toss to mix. Transfer to a serving bowl, sprinkle the remaining cheese over the top, and serve immediately.

NOTE: Fresh, red ripe tomatoes may be substituted for canned. To change the taste, add strips of peppers or cheese, sliced pepperoni, or chopped olives. Do your own thing!

Turkey Twist Salad

4 to 6 main-course servings

This will be one of your favorite summer main course salads. Sometimes I add fresh dill, basil, or garlic—and any pasta shape you have on hand works fine.

- 8 ounces macaroni twists
- 2½ cups smoked turkey (about 12 ounces), cut into ½-inch cubes
- 8 ounces sliced Swiss cheese, cut into thin strips
- 1 cup thinly sliced celery
- 1 cup mayonnaise
- ¼ cup chopped scallions
- 2 tablespoons diced pimiento (optional)
- ¼ cup chopped pecans
- 1 tablespoon prepared mustard
- 1 teaspoon salt
- ½ teaspoon pepper

In a large pot of boiling water, cook macaroni just until tender. Drain, rinse under cold running water, drain well, and put into a large bowl. Add all remaining ingredients and toss to mix well. Cover and refrigerate overnight to blend flavors.

NOTE: You can garnish this with pimiento strips and pecan halves.

VEGGIES

Momma was right when she said, "Eat your veggies, they're good for you." She must have known something, because the health community is now saying the same thing. It's easy to enjoy our veggies now, too, 'cause produce is better than ever. We're eating vegetables fresh, crisp-cooked, mixed in, and at every time of day. Want more ways with them? OK. Here are some of the most requested recipes from my TV show that turn vegetables into "excitement."

TIDBIT: Contrary to what you may have done in the past, you should always store tomatoes out of the refrigerator. If you want them to be juicier, sweeter, and better-textured, they should *never, never, never* be kept in the cold. Keep them on the kitchen counter, stem-side up, until they're really a full, red ripe and you'll enjoy them a lot more. They'll be more like homegrown tomatoes. Remember—tomatoes . . . delicious . . . *never, never, never* in the fridge.

Here's an easy way to peel fresh tomatoes: Remove the stems, dip tomatoes in boiling water for about 15 seconds, then plunge them into cold water; the skins will slip off easily. But be careful: Don't burn yourself when removing the tomatoes from the boiling water.

Zucchini Squares

6 to 8 servings

We're always looking for something new, easy, and interesting to do with all that end-of-the-summer zucchini. This one will surely be the number one rave of the zucchini season. (And the zucchini season is now every season!)

4 eggs

½ cup grated Parmesan cheese

½ cup chopped onion

½ teaspoon seasoned salt

½ teaspoon dried oregano

½ teaspoon garlic powder

¼ cup chopped fresh parsley or 2 tablespoons dried parsley flakes

½ cup vegetable oil

½ cup whole wheat flour

1 cup biscuit baking mix

3 cups grated zucchini

Preheat oven to 375°F. In a large bowl, beat the eggs, add all the remaining ingredients, and mix well. Pour mixture into an ungreased 9-inch square baking pan and bake for 30 to 35 minutes. To brown top, put under preheated broiler for the last 2 or 3 minutes. Cool for a few minutes, then cut into squares.

NOTE: If you have the time, give it a zip with chopped fresh garlic instead of garlic powder.

Crustless Vegetable Pie

6 servings

Great idea for lunch, brunch, or a light main dish at dinner. This turns your favorite veggies into a crustless pie that spins the mystery of what to serve into a whole bunch of hoorays! (This is also super for some of those leftover "bottom-of-the-vegetable-bin-and-starting-to-go-soft" veggies.)

¼ cup vegetable oil

1 small eggplant, peeled and cut into ½-inch cubes

2 medium-sized zucchini, cut into ½-inch cubes

1 medium-sized onion, coarsely chopped

4 medium-sized fresh tomatoes, peeled and chopped, or 1 can (14½ ounces) whole tomatoes, drained

3 eggs

¾ cup grated Parmesan cheese

1 tablespoon minced fresh parsley

½ teaspoon dried basil

½ teaspoon dried oregano

Salt and pepper to taste

1 cup (4 ounces) mozzarella cheese, thinly sliced or shredded

In a large skillet, heat the oil; sauté the eggplant, zucchini, and onion for 7 to 10 minutes, until vegetables are softened. Add the tomatoes; cover and simmer for 20 to 25 minutes, until mixture is quite soft. (If using canned tomatoes, reduce cooking time to 10 minutes.) Transfer to a large bowl and let cool. Preheat oven to 350°F. In a small bowl, beat

the eggs; beat in ¼ cup of the Parmesan cheese, the parsley, basil, and oregano. Add the cheese mixture to the sautéed vegetables; season with salt and pepper. Pour half the mixture into a greased 10-inch pie pan and sprinkle another ¼ cup Parmesan cheese over the top. Add remaining vegetable mixture and then the remaining Parmesan cheese. Top with the mozzarella and bake for 40 to 45 minutes or until set and golden brown.

Better Baked Beans

5 to 6 servings

Simple home-style food—you've got it in these baked beans. Ah-ha! Wait 'til you see how simple. It turns canned baked beans into a world of richness.

1 cup (4 ounces) diced cooked ham or smoked turkey

½ teaspoon dry mustard

¼ cup firmly packed brown sugar

2 tablespoons finely chopped onion

1 cup pineapple chunks in heavy syrup, drained (reserve syrup)

2 cans (1 pound each) pork and beans, or vegetarian beans

Preheat oven to 350°F. Grease a 1½-quart baking dish. In a large bowl, combine the ham, mustard, brown sugar, onion, pineapple, and ¼ cup reserved pineapple syrup. Spoon 1 can of beans into the baking dish. Spoon pineapple mixture over the beans; top with the remaining can of beans. Bake for 55 to 60 minutes or until brown and bubbly on top.

Vegetable Stew

8 to 10 servings

This is one of my favorites as a side dish with anything anytime, but it's also a one-pot supper if you want. It's certainly hearty enough. This will get thicker if you cook it a little longer—or if you make it a day ahead and reheat it.

1 **package (16 ounces) frozen chopped broccoli, partially thawed**

1 **package (10 ounces) frozen Fordhook lima beans, partially thawed**

1 **package (10 ounces) frozen cauliflower, partially thawed**

8 **tablespoons (1 stick) butter or margarine, softened**

2 **cans (10¾ ounces each) chicken broth**

1 **can (14½ ounces) whole tomatoes**

4 **tablespoons instant potato flakes**

4 **tablespoons small-sized pasta, such as *acine de pepe* or *rosa marina***

½ **teaspoon pepper**

Preheat oven to 350°F. In a 9″x13″ baking dish, mix the partially thawed vegetables with the butter. Bake for 15 minutes, turning occasionally to blend butter and vegetables. Meanwhile, combine the chicken broth and tomatoes in a large saucepan and bring to a simmer. Stir in the instant potato flakes, pasta, and pepper. Pour evenly over the vegetables. Bake for an additional 40 to 45 minutes until vegetables are tender.

Smoky Barbecue Bean Bake

8 to 10 servings

They'll come back for seconds and thirds when you serve this down-home taste treat! It's as if you're stirring things up at the old chuck wagon.

4 cans (1 pound each) great Northern or navy beans, drained

2¾ cups mild barbecue sauce

1¼ cups dry bread crumbs

1 pound cooked ham, pork, or smoked turkey, diced

1 large green bell pepper, finely chopped

1 large onion, finely chopped

½ teaspoon liquid smoke

1 cup (4 ounces) shredded Cheddar cheese

3 tablespoons crumbled cooked bacon or imitation bacon bits (optional)

Preheat oven to 375°F. In a large bowl, combine the beans, barbecue sauce, bread crumbs, diced meat, green pepper, onion, and liquid smoke. Put mixture in a greased 9"x13" glass baking dish. Top with the shredded cheese and crumbled bacon. Bake for 35 to 40 minutes.

NOTE: Liquid smoke is usually found in supermarket condiment sections.

Broccoli Pancakes

about 12 small pancakes

Even the non–broccoli eaters love this one 'cause it's in a new-old favorite form. You can also make this with chopped spinach, green beans, or mashed, cooked cauli-flower instead of broccoli.

1½ **cups chopped fresh broccoli or 1 package (10 ounces) frozen chopped broccoli, thawed and drained**

½ **cup pancake or biscuit baking mix**

1 **egg**

¼ **teaspoon salt**

Vegetable oil for frying

If using fresh broccoli, boil or steam it for 3 to 5 minutes just until crisp-tender. Plunge it immediately into a bowl of cold water to keep it crisp. Drain in a strainer, pressing out excess water with the back of a spoon. Combine the pancake mix, egg, and salt in a large bowl; mix well. Mix in drained broccoli. Heat 1 to 2 tablespoons oil in a large skillet. Drop mixture by spoonfuls (about 2 tablespoons per pancake) into hot oil, being careful not to crowd pan. Cook for 2 to 3 minutes on each side, or until golden brown. Repeat with remaining batter, adding more oil to the pan if necessary. Serve warm or cold.

Corn Pudding

4 servings

Here's how those few extra ears of corn you made for supper become the reason for making a few extra the next time—and when fresh corn season is over, try it with frozen or even canned corn. A nice dinner side dish—they're guaranteed to love it.

2 cups corn kernels	2 eggs, beaten
1 teaspoon sugar	1 cup milk
1 teaspoon vanilla extract	1 tablespoon butter or margarine
1 teaspoon salt	2 tablespoons cracker crumbs
¼ teaspoon pepper	

Preheat oven to 350°F. Mix all ingredients together in a large bowl. Pour into a 1½-quart ungreased casserole dish. Set casserole dish in a large baking pan, and add hot water to pan to come about halfway up the outside of the casserole dish. Bake for 60 to 70 minutes, until set.

NOTE: Use either saltines or Ritz®-type crackers to make crumbs.

Sweet Onion Casserole

8 to 10 servings

This takes plain old onions and so easily turns them into a throw-together, perfect side dish for any main course. So what if you decide on your side dish first and then worry about what you're gonna buy at the market for the "biggie"? Maybe add a little zip by adding barbecue-flavored chips, or sprinkle in some tarragon for a French taste or some oregano for tilting it toward Italy, or . . . whatever you want.

- 2 cans (10¾ ounces each) condensed cream of mushroom soup
- ½ cup milk
- 4 medium-sized Spanish onions, sliced into ¼-inch rings
- 2 cups (8 ounces) grated Cheddar cheese
- 1 package (10 ounces) potato chips, crushed
- ½ teaspoon salt
- Pepper to taste
- Paprika

Preheat oven to 350°F. Blend the soup and milk in a small bowl; season with salt and pepper. Arrange half the onion rings in the bottom of a greased 9″x13″ baking dish. Cover with half the cheese, then half the potato chips. Repeat layers. Pour the soup mixture over layers. Cover and bake for 1 hour. Sprinkle with paprika.

Sunny Slaw

4 to 6 servings

Coleslaw is an almost universal dish, and everybody has his or her own way of making it. If you've got a favorite, fine. But here's a simple one that works every time!

½ medium-sized green cabbage, shredded, *or* 6 cups shredded green cabbage

1 cup shredded carrots

DRESSING

⅓ cup white vinegar

¼ cup sugar

¼ cup vegetable oil

2 teaspoons salt

2 tablespoons grated or minced onion

Mix all the dressing ingredients together in a small bowl. Put the shredded cabbage in a large bowl, pour the dressing over, and toss. Put the slaw in a salad bowl and arrange the shredded carrots around the slaw to form a border.

reamy Coleslaw

8 to 10 servings

Prefer the creamy type of coleslaw? Well, here's a recipe you'll love.

1 medium-sized green cabbage, coarsely chopped, or 12 cups shredded green cabbage

3 carrots, coarsely grated or chopped

2 green bell peppers, seeded and coarsely grated or chopped

½ cup sliced scallions

DRESSING

1 cup mayonnaise

⅓ cup lemon juice

½ cup buttermilk

¼ cup sugar

2 teaspoons vinegar

1 teaspoon dry mustard

¼ teaspoon cayenne pepper

Salt and black pepper to taste

1 can (8 ounces) pineapple chunks in natural juice, drained (optional)

In a large bowl, combine the cabbage, carrots, peppers, and scallions. In a medium-sized bowl, whisk together all the dressing ingredients. Pour the dressing over the cabbage mixture, add pineapple, and toss to coat. Chill for at least 1 hour.

Garlic Green Salad

4 servings

Here's a quickie that's not only a salad, but also a super snack to have on hand. Watch it disappear! I like to add the broccoli stems, also, so I peel them, cut them into ½-inch slices, and cook them with the rest of the broccoli. Green beans work well, too—or maybe try a combination of green beans and broccoli.

½ cup mayonnaise

2 tablespoons sour cream

2 garlic cloves, chopped, or 2 teaspoons bottled chopped garlic

½ teaspoon salt

¼ teaspoon pepper

1 large bunch broccoli, cut into medium-sized florets, or 2 packages (10 ounces each) frozen broccoli spears, thawed and cut into 1-inch pieces

Grated lemon or lime rind for garnish

In a large bowl, mix together the mayonnaise, sour cream, garlic, salt, and pepper. Boil or steam the broccoli for 5 to 6 minutes (3 to 4 minutes for frozen broccoli), just until crisp-tender. Plunge the broccoli into a bowl of cold water to stop the cooking and to retain its bright green color. Drain well. Add broccoli to the mayonnaise/sour cream mixture. Refrigerate until chilled. Garnish with lemon or lime rind.

Vegetable Stuffed Peppers

6 servings

This is super beautiful next to your main course, super easy to serve because it's the "holder" and the vegetable all in one. When fresh corn isn't available, I use frozen or canned. You might try broccoli instead of the green beans. You can even turn this into a whole meal by adding some cooked rice or some cubed cooked turkey or chicken.

6 medium-sized green bell peppers

4 tablespoons (¼ cup) butter or margarine

½ cup chopped onion

2 cups cooked corn kernels

2 cups cooked cut green beans

2 medium-sized fresh tomatoes, chopped

1 teaspoon salt

Pepper to taste

1 cup (4 ounces) grated Cheddar cheese

Preheat oven to 350°F. Wash the peppers; slice off tops and remove seeds. In a large pot of boiling salted water, cook peppers for 5 minutes; drain well. In a small skillet, sauté onion in butter for 4 to 5 minutes, just until soft. In a large bowl, mix the corn, green beans, tomatoes, salt, and pepper; stir in the onion. Fill peppers with the vegetable mixture; sprinkle the grated cheese on top. Place stuffed peppers in an ungreased baking dish and bake for 25 to 30 minutes, until peppers are tender and vegetables are heated through.

Marinated Carrots

10 to 12 servings

Better than sweet-and-sour, better than pickled, better than buttered. There isn't anybody who doesn't love carrots this way, and if you think this is sensational as a cold dish, try it as a hot dish. All you do is put it in a baking dish and heat it 'til it's warmed through; couldn't be easier—and besides, with reheating, it gets better every time.

5 cups frozen sliced carrots (a 20-ounce bag is 3 cups)

1 medium-sized onion, thinly sliced

1 small green bell pepper, cut into slivers

½ cup sugar

1 can (10 ounces) tomato soup

½ cup vegetable oil

½ cup white vinegar

1 teaspoon Worcestershire sauce

3 tablespoons prepared mustard

1 teaspoon salt

¼ teaspoon pepper

In a large saucepan, cook the carrots in salted water until they are crisp-tender. Drain and let cool. In a large bowl, mix the onion and green pepper. Add remaining ingredients and mix well. Add carrots and toss to coat. Cover and marinate in refrigerator for at least 12 hours or overnight. Drain off marinade and serve.

NOTE: Even easier? Use canned carrots—then there's no cooking at all. It's just mixing. Yippee!

Greek Cucumber Salad

3 to 4 servings

How about this Greek variation of cucumber salad? It's a snap! It tastes like when Momma used to take summer cukes and throw them together like this just to use them up. Remember how we gobbled them up?

- 3 medium-sized cucumbers, peeled (and seeded if desired) and cut into ½-inch cubes
- 1 cup (8 ounces) plain yogurt or sour cream
- 1 tablespoon olive oil
- 1 teaspoon white wine vinegar
- ½ teaspoon salt
- ⅛ teaspoon pepper
- 1 garlic clove, minced, or ¼ teaspoon garlic powder
- 1½ teaspoons chopped fresh dill *or* ½ teaspoon dried dillweed
- 2 tablespoons chopped scallions
- ¼ to ½ teaspoon sugar (to taste)

Combine all ingredients in a large bowl. Cover and chill for at least one hour. Stir well before serving.

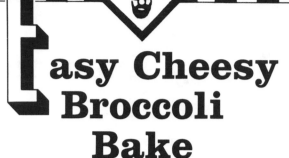

Easy Cheesy Broccoli Bake

4 to 6 servings

We're always looking to make something new or different with broccoli 'cause it's so popular right now. Well, try this. It's not too new or different but just the way you'll like it. Oh yes, you can use cream of mushroom or cream of chicken soup instead of cream of celery soup if that's handier. And if you use frozen broccoli just let it thaw— you don't even have to cook it first.

1 large bunch broccoli (about 1½ pounds), separated into stalks	½ cup (2 ounces) shredded sharp Cheddar cheese
1 can (10¾ ounces) condensed cream of celery soup	¼ cup seasoned bread crumbs, tossed with 1 tablespoon melted butter
⅓ cup milk	

Preheat oven to 350°F. Boil or steam broccoli for just a few minutes, so it stays crunchy. Meanwhile, in a medium-sized bowl, blend the soup, milk, and Cheddar cheese. Drain broccoli and arrange in an ungreased shallow 6"x10" baking dish. Pour soup mixture over broccoli. Top with bread crumbs. Bake for 25 to 30 minutes, or until hot and bubbly.

Easy Stewed Tomatoes

about 4 cups

Here's a sure-fire family favorite with down-home good-ness that tastes better than the "store-bought" kind. And wait 'til they ask how you made them!

- 6 to 8 fresh, very ripe tomatoes, peeled, or 1 can (28 ounces) whole tomatoes
- 3 tablespoons butter or margarine
- 1 tablespoon lemon juice
- 1 tablespoon sugar
- 1½ teaspoons salt
- ¼ teaspoon pepper
- ½ green bell pepper, chopped
- 2 cups crumbled bread (any kind)
- 1 tablespoon diced onion (optional)

Put tomatoes in a large deep skillet. Cook over medium heat, stirring occasionally, for 10 to 15 minutes. Add all the remaining ingredients and cook until thick, stirring occasionally. Serve it hot as a side dish.

NOTE: I use canned tomatoes most of the time 'cause it's so much easier, but if you've got a lot of fresh "starting-to-go-soft" tomatoes around, this will turn them into great tomatoes.

Crunchy Broccoli

4 to 6 servings

This does it when you want broccoli a fast "today-popular" way. It's crunchy and delicious. In fact, any veggie or combination of veggies, fresh or frozen, can be served this way.

3 tablespoons olive oil

1 garlic clove, crushed

2 packages (10 ounces each) frozen broccoli spears, thawed

½ cup grated Parmesan or Romano cheese

In a large skillet, heat olive oil over medium-high heat; add the garlic and broccoli and sauté just until crisp-tender. Arrange broccoli on a serving dish and sprinkle with the cheese.

Mock Crabmeat Salad

4 servings

It will be the conversation piece of the party: parsnips in a mock crabmeat salad. That's right—people will discover how smart you are!

- 2 cups shredded or grated parsnips (about 1½ pounds)
- 8 green or black olives, chopped
- 1 pimiento, chopped
- 1 cup diced celery
- 1 onion, grated or minced
- Salt and pepper to taste
- Thousand Island dressing or mayonnaise to moisten
- Lettuce leaves

In a large bowl, mix the parsnips, olives, pimiento, celery, onion, salt, and pepper. Mix in dressing or mayonnaise to your taste. Refrigerate until chilled. Serve on lettuce leaves.

Bean Chili

8 to 10 servings

Chili is so popular because it's so good. Here's a meatless one you'll really enjoy.

- 1 large onion, chopped
- 2 tablespoons olive oil
- 1 cup picante sauce
- 1 cup chicken broth
- 2 cans (28 ounces each) crushed tomatoes or 2 cans (28 ounces each) whole tomatoes, chopped
- 1 can (15 ounces) pinto beans, drained
- 1 can (15 ounces) kidney beans, drained
- 1 can (15 ounces) black-eyed peas, drained
- 1 teaspoon ground cumin

In a large saucepan or Dutch oven, sauté the onion in the olive oil for 4 to 5 minutes, until softened. Add all the remaining ingredients, bring to a boil, reduce heat and simmer for 10 to 12 minutes.

NOTE: Served with a salad this is a whole meal, but it's also a great go-along. You can add some browned meat or sausage, a little salt or garlic to give it a "tang," or even any combination of beans.

BREADS AND MUFFINS

Nothing says "homemade" louder than breads and muffins. Put a few homemades in a basket to make the meal jump steps higher. And they're easy, too. Well, most of the ones that I make are easy. They're just mixing and baking. There's no kneading and rolling and proofing and time, time, time to clean up the kitchen—Who needs that today? These are more cakey-type breads, so cut thick slices and you'll remember the taste of way back when. Enjoy!

Apple Cinnamon Rolls

16 rolls

These fit every occasion, from a snack to Thanksgiving dinner. Try serving them with whipped cream (super!), or ice cream (super, again!), or Cheddar cheese (double super!!). And starting with a bought pastry dough makes it twice as gourmet-looking but twice as easy.

1 teaspoon ground cinnamon

½ cup sugar

1 can (8 ounces) refrigerated crescent rolls

2 large apples (golden delicious or Granny Smith), peeled, cored, and each cut into 8 wedges

2 tablespoons butter or margarine, melted

¼ cup orange juice or water

Preheat oven to 400°F. In a small bowl, mix the cinnamon and sugar together. Unroll crescent roll dough; separate into 8 triangles. Cut each in half lengthwise to make 16 triangular strips. Place an apple wedge on the wide end of each strip; roll up. Arrange rolls in a 9"x13" baking dish. Drizzle with the melted butter; sprinkle with cinnamon-sugar mixture. Pour orange juice or water into baking dish, but not over rolls. Bake for 30 to 35 minutes or until rolls are golden brown and apple wedges are tender.

California Fig–Oat Bran Muffins

12 muffins

Oats—they're all the rage, so here's a simple, delicious muffin that's also very, very healthy. It looks difficult 'cause there are a lot of ingredients, but they're simple ingredients and if you get them all ready first, then all you do is throw them together and mix. Don't tell anyone, but I still like to spread on a little butter or margarine.

- 1½ cups oat, whole wheat, or unbleached all-purpose flour
- ½ cup oatmeal (rolled oats), regular or instant
- 1 teaspoon ground cinnamon
- 1½ teaspoons baking soda
- 2 teaspoons baking powder
- 1½ cups bran flakes cereal
- ½ cup apple juice
- 3 tablespoons cholesterol-free egg substitute or 1 egg
- ½ cup low-fat milk
- 1 can (6 ounces) frozen apple juice concentrate, thawed
- 3 tablespoons vegetable oil
- 1 large banana, mashed
- ¾ cup finely chopped dried California figs
- 2 tablespoons honey or ¼ cup firmly packed brown sugar

Preheat oven to 350° F. Line a muffin pan with paper baking cups. In a medium-sized bowl, mix the flour, oatmeal, cinnamon, baking soda, and baking powder. Combine the bran flakes and apple juice in a large bowl; stir well to moisten the flakes evenly. Add the egg substitute, milk, apple juice concentrate, oil, banana, figs, and honey. Mix well. Stir in the flour mixture and mix well. Spoon batter into muffin cups, distributing evenly. Bake for 20 to 25 minutes or until toothpick inserted into center of muffins comes out clean.

NOTE: Sure, you can use any figs, but the California ones are more plump and moist.

Quick and Moist Bread

1 round loaf

No proofing, rising, or punching down here. This bread is just mix and bake—SO EASY! The smell of freshly baked bread in the house will drive everyone wild.

5 cups self-rising flour	1 can (12 ounces) beer
5 tablespoons sugar	Melted butter or margarine
1½ cups (12 ounces) sour cream	

Preheat oven to 350°F. In a large bowl, combine the flour and sugar. Add the sour cream and beer alternately; mix well. Pour batter into a greased 2-quart round baking dish. Bake for 45 minutes; brush top with butter. Bake for 15 to 20 minutes more or until toothpick inserted into the center comes out clean. Let cool slightly; serve warm, cool, or sliced and toasted.

Easy Herbed Onion Bread

1 loaf

There's no punching, no rolling, no kneading, no big mess when you make this bread. There's nothing to it. And with the dill and basil it yells "Homemade!" The family will love this easy, cakey bread—so will company and neighbors—and everybody!

- 1½ cups finely chopped Spanish onions
- 2 tablespoons butter or margarine
- 3 cups biscuit baking mix
- 1 egg
- 1 cup milk
- 1 teaspoon dried basil
- 1 teaspoon dried dillweed

Preheat oven to 350°F. In a large skillet, sauté the onion in the butter for 5 to 7 minutes, until tender. Meanwhile, combine all remaining ingredients in a large bowl. Add onions, mixing just until blended. Spoon into a greased 9"x5" loaf pan. Bake for 55 to 60 minutes, until golden. Cool before removing from pan.

Strawberry Nut Bread

2 loaves

Show off strawberries no matter what the season. If you like, chop up some fresh berries and add them to the batter, or top the finished breads with fresh berries and whipped cream. That's like a double berry shortcake with berries soaked into the cake. Take a look at how easy it is.

- 2 cups all-purpose flour
- 1 cup sugar
- 1 teaspoon baking soda
- ½ teaspoon salt
- ½ teaspoon ground cinnamon
- ½ teaspoon nutmeg

- 3 eggs, at room temperature
- 1 cup vegetable oil
- 1 cup strawberry-flavored dessert topping
- 1 cup chopped walnuts

Preheat oven to 350°F. Grease two 8"x4" loaf pans. Thoroughly mix all ingredients together in a large bowl. Divide mixture in half and pour into loaf pans. Bake for 1 hour or until toothpick inserted into center comes out clean. Cool in pans on wire racks for 10 minutes. Remove from pans and cool thoroughly on racks before slicing.

NOTE: Serve with butter, margarine, or cream cheese.

Pumpkin Nut Bread

3 loaves

This proves that pumpkin isn't only for Halloween. It's a rich, homemade taste for anytime.

4 eggs	2 teaspoons baking soda
3 cups sugar	1½ teaspoons salt
1 cup peanut oil	1 teaspoon ground cinnamon
⅓ cup water	1½ cups chopped dates
1 can (30 ounces) pumpkin pie mix	1 cup chopped roasted peanuts
3½ cups all-purpose flour	

Preheat oven to 350°F. Grease and flour three 9"x5" loaf pans. In a large bowl, lightly beat the eggs. Gradually beat in the sugar, oil, water, and pumpkin. Add the flour, baking soda, salt, and cinnamon; mix well. Stir in the dates and peanuts. Divide the batter evenly among the loaf pans. Bake for 55 minutes to 1 hour or until the bread begins to pull away from the sides of the pans. Cool in pans on wire racks for 30 minutes, then remove from pans and cool completely on racks.

NOTE: Sometimes I use raisins instead of dates, or even some of both.

Sweet Potato Bread

3 loaves

Keep the extra loaves in the freezer for whenever company pops over. That way, you're always prepared.

3½ cups all-purpose flour

2 teaspoons baking soda

½ teaspoon salt

1 teaspoon ground cinnamon

1 teaspoon ground nutmeg

3 cups sugar

1 cup vegetable oil

4 eggs

⅔ cup water

2 cups cooked mashed sweet potatoes (about 4 large yams)

1 cup chopped nuts (optional)

Preheat oven to 350°F. In a large bowl, mix the flour, baking soda, salt, cinnamon, and nutmeg. In another large bowl, combine the sugar and oil; beat well. Beat in the eggs. Add the flour mixture and water alternately. Stir in the sweet potatoes and chopped nuts. Divide the batter evenly among three greased 9"x5" loaf pans. Bake for 1 hour or until toothpick inserted into center of loaves comes out clean. Cool in pans on rack.

Applesauce Bread

1 loaf

What a nice, moist bread this is! It's perfect just as is for a snack or topped with some whipped cream or ice cream for a fancier dessert for company. . . . Mmmmmm!!

2 cups whole wheat flour	½ teaspoon ground nutmeg
1 teaspoon baking soda	1½ cups applesauce
½ teaspoon baking powder	⅔ cup sugar
1 teaspoon ground cinnamon	¼ cup vegetable oil
	2 eggs
	¼ cup milk

Preheat oven to 350°F. Sift together the flour, baking soda, baking powder, cinnamon, and nutmeg. In a large bowl, combine the applesauce, sugar, oil, eggs, and milk; mix well. Add the dry ingredients and beat well. Pour into a greased 9"x5" loaf pan. Bake for 1 hour or until toothpick inserted into center comes out clean. Remove from pan; cool on wire rack.

NOTE: I like it a little sweeter, so I add an additional ⅓ cup sugar. You can also use skim milk instead of regular.

Quick Sticky Bun Muffins

4 servings

Here's the answer to what you're gonna have with your coffee or milk—or with last-minute company or anyone you want to share a 15-minute fresh, warm party with!

2 tablespoons butter or margarine	2 tablespoons raisins
¼ cup firmly packed brown sugar	¼ teaspoon ground cinnamon
¼ cup light or dark corn syrup	2 English muffins, split
¼ cup chopped nuts (walnuts or pecans)	

Preheat oven to 400°F. Melt the butter in an 8-inch round cake pan. Stir in the brown sugar, corn syrup, nuts, raisins, and cinnamon. Arrange the English muffin halves cut-side down on top of the syrup mixture. Bake for 15 minutes or until bubbly. Immediately invert the muffins onto a serving dish and serve.

Cheese Corn Mini-Muffins

36 mini-muffins

This is my type of baking—just mixing. Try serving these with a garlic spread or a chili or jalapeño spread. Even plain butter will taste extra special topping these.

- 1 cup yellow corn-meal
- 1 cup all-purpose flour
- ½ cup shredded Jarlsberg cheese
- ¼ cup sugar
- 2 tablespoons minced green bell pepper
- 2 tablespoons minced red bell pepper
- 2 teaspoons baking powder
- 1½ teaspoons salt
- 1 cup (8 ounces) sour cream
- 2 eggs
- 4 tablespoons (¼ cup) butter or margarine, melted

Preheat oven to 425°F. In a large bowl, combine the corn-meal, flour, cheese, sugar, peppers, baking powder, and salt; mix well. In another large bowl, beat together the sour cream, eggs, and butter. Stir in the dry ingredients and mix well. Divide mixture evenly among 3 generously greased mini-muffin pans, filling cups almost to the top. Bake for 10 to 15 minutes or until golden. Cool in pans on a wire rack for 5 minutes. Serve warm.

NOTE: Be sure to check out the Chili Cheese Butter!

Chili Cheese Butter

1 cup

Enjoy this spread—it's great with the Cheese Corn Muffins. (You'll probably find other things to serve it with, too!)

- 8 tablespoons (1 stick) butter or margarine, softened
- ½ cup (2 ounces) shredded Jarlsberg cheese
- 1 small garlic clove, minced
- ¼ teaspoon chili powder

Combine all ingredients in a medium-sized bowl; mix well. Spoon into serving dish; cover and refrigerate until ready to serve.

NOTE: If Jarlsberg cheese is not available, any Swiss cheese will do.

Applesauce 'n' Spice Bread

1 loaf

Make a couple of these and put some in the freezer. It's my kind of baking: simple and no-fail, plus it tastes like it's right from the tree with a crunchy outside and moist inside. Great for a bring-along gift, too. And at holiday time when you don't wanna go empty-handed? These will do the trick for sure.

2 cups all-purpose flour

1 teaspoon baking soda

½ teaspoon baking powder

¼ teaspoon salt

½ teaspoon ground cinnamon

¼ teaspoon ground nutmeg

¼ teaspoon ground allspice

1 cup sugar

½ cup vegetable oil

1¼ cups applesauce

2 eggs

3 tablespoons milk

½ cup coarsely chopped pecans

TOPPING

¼ cup chopped pecans

¼ cup firmly packed brown sugar

½ teaspoon ground cinnamon

Preheat oven to 350°F. Sift together the flour, baking soda, baking powder, salt, and spices. In a large bowl, combine the sugar, oil, applesauce, eggs, and milk. Stir the dry ingredients into the applesauce mixture; stir in the ½ cup pecans. Pour batter into a greased 9"x5" loaf pan. Mix topping ingredients thoroughly and sprinkle over batter. Bake for 1 to 1¼ hours or until toothpick inserted into center comes out clean. Cool in pan.

Quick Rolls

12 rolls

These are easy—no rolling and no proofing! But they still give you bragging rights for being homemade.

2 cups self-rising flour	4 tablespoons mayonnaise
1 cup milk	1 tablespoon sugar

Preheat oven to 450°F. In a large bowl, stir together all ingredients to form a soft dough. Spoon into a well-greased 12-cup muffin pan, distributing evenly. Bake for 10 to 12 minutes, until golden brown.

NOTE: Be sure to use whole milk only.

Fresh Apple Cinnamon Muffins

12 muffins

See how easy it can be to put that extra special touch into a bread basket?

1½ cups all-purpose flour

⅓ cup sugar

2 teaspoons baking powder

½ teaspoon ground cinnamon

½ teaspoon salt

1 egg

½ cup milk

1 medium apple, peeled, cored, and finely chopped

4 tablespoons (¼ cup) butter or margarine, melted

TOPPING

⅓ cup chopped nuts (walnuts or pecans)

¼ cup firmly packed brown sugar

½ teaspoon ground cinnamon

Preheat oven to 375°F. In a large bowl, combine the flour, sugar, baking powder, ½ teaspoon cinnamon, and salt. In a medium-sized bowl, beat together the egg and milk. Stir in the chopped apple and melted butter. Add all at once to flour mixture; stir just until mixed (batter will be very stiff). Spoon into a greased muffin pan, filling each cup about two-thirds full. Mix topping ingredients thoroughly and sprinkle over each muffin. Bake for 15 to 20 minutes. Remove from pan immediately and serve warm.

DESSERTS

The number one food desire no matter where, when, or how is dessert. We'll do without something else, as long as we can have dessert. Without a doubt, I get more requests for dessert recipes than anything else. Why, dessert is the titillating part of the meal, bordering on sinful. You know the excitement, the oohs and aahs that happen when dessert is served. And dessert doesn't have to be fancy, it just has to be something we love. For instance, everybody loves ice cream, and served plain it's super enough. But put some chocolate sauce on it or some hot fudge, and watch your friends multiply. No chocolate sauce? Break up a chocolate bar over it and immediately you've made it even more down-home comfortable. See, it doesn't take much.

In this chapter we've got apple cakes and filled cupcakes and cheesecake pies and chocolate desserts and frozen desserts and . . . well, just take a look. There's something to fit every time and every place, from fancy to just thrown together and sprinkled "on top of." Every one of them is as easy as can be, fancy looking but not "fancy costing," so we don't have to spend a lot of time and money. Everybody's happy, including us. So for that snack or "just what you wanted" topper to your meal, read on, read on!

Crustless Cheesecake

6 to 8 servings

Easy as can be, great taste, and great looks, too. This is still an all-time favorite with everybody. It was my very first overwhelming hit recipe. There's a reason and you'll know it when you taste it and serve it. It can't be this easy? Oh, yes it can!

2 packages (8 ounces each) cream cheese, softened

⅔ cup sugar

3 eggs

½ teaspoon vanilla extract

¼ teaspoon fresh lemon juice

TOPPING

2 cups (16 ounces) sour cream

3 tablespoons sugar

1 teaspoon vanilla extract

¼ teaspoon fresh lemon juice

Preheat oven to 325°F. Put the cream cheese and sugar in a large bowl and beat well. Beat in the eggs, one at a time. Beat in the vanilla and lemon juice. Spoon mixture into a greased 9-inch glass pie plate. Bake for 45 to 50 minutes, until golden brown. Remove from oven and let cool for 10 to 15 minutes. (Do not turn off oven.) Meanwhile, mix all topping ingredients together. Spread over the top of the cheesecake and bake for 10 minutes longer (the top will remain almost liquid). Let cool, then refrigerate for 4 hours or overnight.

NOTE: I like to cover the cheesecake with some of my favorite pie filling before serving it.

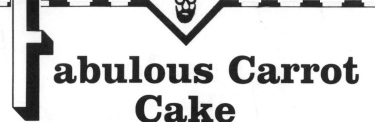

abulous Carrot Cake

20 servings

Carrot cake became newly popular in the 60's, but it's been around since pioneer days. And no wonder—it's great for snacking, for company, with or without frosting, any time, any way. Here's an easy one that comes out moist and rich. The frosting is a super traditional cream cheese topping, but the cake is just as yummy served plain!

- 3 cups all-purpose flour
- 2 teaspoons baking soda
- 1 teaspoon ground cinnamon
- 1 teaspoon ground ginger
- ½ teaspoon salt
- ½ pound (2 sticks) butter, softened
- 1 cup firmly packed brown sugar
- 1 cup granulated sugar
- 4 eggs
- 1 can (20 ounces) crushed pineapple in heavy syrup, drained well

- 1 pound carrots, shredded
- 1 cup raisins
- 2 teaspoons vanilla extract

SILKY FROSTING

- 1 package (8 ounces) cream cheese, softened
- 8 tablespoons (1 stick) butter, softened
- 1 teaspoon fresh grated lemon peel
- 1 tablespoon lemon juice
- 1½ cups sifted confectioners' sugar

Preheat the oven to 350°F. Grease and flour a 9″x13″ baking pan. In a large bowl, combine the flour, baking soda, cinnamon, ginger, and salt. In another large bowl, cream the butter and sugars until light and fluffy. Beat in the eggs, one at a time. Beat in the pineapple, carrots, raisins, and vanilla extract. Gradually beat in the flour mixture until well blended. Pour into prepared baking pan. Bake for 50 to 60 minutes, until toothpick inserted in center comes out clean. Let cool completely in pan. To make the frosting, in a large bowl, beat together the cream cheese and butter until light and fluffy. Beat in the lemon peel and juice. Gradually beat in sugar until smooth. Spread over the cooled cake.

French Coffee Cake

10 to 12 servings

This will look as if you fussed but it's as easy as a mix. And everybody'll love it, so it's great for entertaining family or friends.

FILLING/TOPPING
- ½ cup firmly packed light brown sugar
- 2 tablespoons all-purpose flour
- ½ cup chopped walnuts
- 1 cup chocolate chips
- 1 teaspoon ground cinnamon

CAKE
- 2 cups all-purpose flour
- 1 teaspoon baking powder
- 1 teaspoon baking soda
- ½ teaspoon salt
- 8 tablespoons (1 stick) butter, softened
- 1 cup sugar
- 2 eggs
- 1 cup (8 ounces) sour cream
- 1 teaspoon vanilla extract

Preheat oven to 350°F. Grease and flour a 9-inch round pan with removable bottom. Combine all the filling/topping ingredients, mix well, and set aside. In a medium-sized bowl, mix together the flour, baking powder, baking soda, and salt. In a large bowl, cream the butter and sugar, then beat in the eggs. Beat in the sour cream and vanilla until creamy. Beat in the dry ingredients. Pour half the batter into prepared pan. Sprinkle half the filling/topping mixture over it. Pour in the remaining cake mixture, and top with remaining filling/topping mixture. Bake for 50 to 60 minutes, until a toothpick inserted in cake comes out clean. Let cool in pan for 10 minutes on a wire rack. Remove from pan and place on a serving plate.

NOTE: If you prefer, you can replace the chocolate chips with 8 ounces of chopped figs or ½ cup of your favorite preserves.

Praline Squares

about 30 squares

Want something a little novel, a little special? These keep nicely in a covered container—but they won't be there for long. They seem to disappear for some reason!

24 whole graham crackers	1 cup firmly packed brown sugar
½ pound (2 sticks) butter	1 cup chopped pecans or walnuts

Preheat oven to 350°F. Lay out the crackers so they touch each other in an ungreased 10"x15" baking pan. Put the butter and brown sugar in a small saucepan, bring to a boil over medium heat, and cook, stirring constantly, for 2 minutes. Stir in the nuts; mix well. Spoon mixture over graham crackers. Bake for 10 minutes. Remove from oven and let cool in pan for 2 minutes. Cut into squares while still warm. Store tightly covered.

ce Cream Cone Pie

6 to 8 servings

Remember when you got down to the bottom of your ice cream cone and it was filled with the last of your ice cream and you wished you could start over? Well, that was the best part and so is this. In fact, everyone can enjoy the best part with this creamy, crunchy pie.

12 sugar cones

1 cup coarsely chopped toasted pecans

½ cup chocolate chips

5 tablespoons butter

½ gallon any flavor ice cream, softened

Put the sugar cones in a plastic bag or between sheets of waxed paper and crush into small pieces with a rolling pin. (Do not chop in food processor.) Mix crushed cones and pecans in a medium-sized bowl; set aside. Put the chocolate chips and butter in a small heavy saucepan and melt, stirring occasionally, over low heat. Pour over cone mixture, mixing well. Press one third of the mixture evenly over the bottom and up the sides of an ungreased 9-inch pie plate. Spread half the ice cream over mixture. Sprinkle another third of the crumbs over ice cream, and spread remaining ice cream over crumbs. Sprinkle remaining crumbs over top of pie, and press down crumbs with the back of a spoon. Cover and freeze for several hours or until firm. Pie may be kept frozen for up to 1 month.

NOTE: The secret to success is softening the ice cream before using it and freezing the final product in a good cold freezer. To soften ice cream, break it up in a mixing bowl and stir with a wooden spoon. *Do not let the ice cream reach the melting point.*

Two-Tone Cheese Pie

6 to 8 servings

Want to "fire up" your company without heating up your kitchen? Then you'll love this special recipe, and so will your guests.

- **2 packages (8 ounces each) cream cheese, softened**
- **¼ cup honey**
- **¼ cup sugar**
- **½ cup heavy cream**
- **2 tablespoons vanilla extract**

- **3 tablespoons cocoa**
- **½ cup coarsely chopped almonds**
- **1 baked 9-inch pie shell or prepared 9-inch graham cracker pie crust**

In a medium-sized bowl, combine the cream cheese, honey, sugar, cream, and vanilla; beat until smooth. Pour mixture into 2 smaller bowls. Stir cocoa into one half of the filling; stir the almonds into the other half. Spread cocoa mixture over bottom of pie shell. Pour nut mixture over, spreading evenly. Refrigerate for several hours or overnight.

NOTE: Be sure to use regular cream cheese, not the soft spread or the whipped kind.

Gorgeous Grasshopper Pie

6 to 8 servings

This recipe is great when you want to make a gourmet-looking and gourmet-tasting dessert without the gourmet work. Everyone will be impressed and you'll be the only one who'll know how easy it was to make. It's like a chocolate mint pie.

- 4 tablespoons (¼ cup) butter or margarine
- 2 cups finely crushed cream-filled chocolate sandwich cookies (about 20)
- 1 package (8 ounces) cream cheese, softened
- 1 can (14 ounces) sweetened condensed milk

- 3 tablespoons lemon juice
- ½ cup green crème de menthe
- ¼ cup white crème de cacao
- 1 container (8 ounces) frozen whipped topping, thawed
- Mint leaves or candy mint leaves for garnish (optional)

Melt butter in a small saucepan. Reserve 1 tablespoon cookie crumbs for garnish; stir remaining crumbs into melted butter. Pat crumb mixture firmly over bottom and up sides of a greased 9-inch pie plate. Refrigerate while preparing filling. In a large mixing bowl, beat the cream cheese until fluffy; gradually beat in the sweetened condensed milk. Stir in the lemon juice and liqueurs; fold in the whipped topping. Mound filling into chilled crust; garnish with reserved crumbs and, if desired, mint leaves. Refrigerate for 4 hours or until set.

Millionaire's Pie

6 to 8 servings

Here's another no-bake pie. You may even feel like a millionaire on a tropical vacation in paradise. If you do . . . call me. I'll be right over!

1 envelope (1.3 ounces) whipped topping mix

1 teaspoon vanilla extract

½ cup cold milk

1 can (20 ounces) pineapple chunks in heavy syrup, drained

1 cup chopped pecans

1 can (14 ounces) sweetened condensed milk

Juice of 1 lemon

1 prepared 9-inch graham cracker pie crust

Make the whipped topping according to package directions, using milk and vanilla. Stir in the pineapple, pecans, sweetened condensed milk, and lemon juice; mix well. Pour into graham cracker crust. Chill in refrigerator for at least 1 hour.

Apple Pudding

12 to 15 servings

This is a great way to use those leftover apples at the bottom of the fruit bin, and you'll get applause for being a star.

2 cups all-purpose flour

1 tablespoon ground cinnamon

1 teaspoon ground nutmeg

¼ teaspoon ground allspice

2 teaspoons baking soda

8 tablespoons (1 stick) butter or margarine, softened

2 cups sugar

3 eggs

2 cups milk

5 large apples, peeled, cored, and finely chopped

½ cup chopped pecans, almonds, or walnuts

Preheat oven to 325°F. In a large bowl, mix the flour, cinnamon, nutmeg, allspice, and baking soda together. In another large bowl, cream the softened butter until light and fluffy. Beat in the sugar; beat in the eggs, one at a time. Stir in dry ingredients and the milk alternately. Stir in the chopped apples and nuts. Pour into a greased 9"x13" baking pan. Bake for 55 minutes to 1 hour, or until a toothpick inserted in the center comes out clean. Let cool to room temperature. Cut into squares or spoon into bowls and top with whipped cream or ice cream.

Apple Cake "No Bother"

8 to 12 servings

This is a great way to use apples during apple season. While you've got the apples, why not make a few of these and give them away as house gifts? Everyone will think you went to a lot of trouble (but you'll know it was "no bother" at all). Heck!! Did I say in apple season? Nowadays, it's always apple season.

⅔ cup vegetable oil

2 eggs

3 cups diced (peeled) apple

1½ cups sugar

1¾ cups all-purpose flour

1 teaspoon baking soda

½ teaspoon salt

2 teaspoons ground cinnamon

1 tablespoon vanilla extract

1 cup chopped walnuts or pecans

Preheat oven to 325°F. Grease a 9"x13" baking pan. In a large bowl, beat the oil and eggs until foamy. Stir in the apples and sugar. In another large bowl, mix together the flour, baking soda, salt, and cinnamon; stir the apple mixture into flour mixture, then stir in the vanilla and nuts. Pour into prepared baking pan. Bake for 45 to 50 minutes or until top springs back when touched lightly.

Seven-Layer Cookies

12 to 15 squares

These are great to have around for snacking. They're yummy, chewy, and easy.

- 8 tablespoons (1 stick) butter or margarine, melted
- 1 cup graham cracker crumbs
- 1 cup sweetened flake coconut
- 6 ounces chocolate chips
- 6 ounces peanut butter chips
- 1 can (14 ounces) sweetened condensed milk
- 1½ cups coarsely chopped walnuts

Preheat oven to 350°F. Pour the melted butter into a 9"x13" baking dish. Sprinkle the crumbs over bottom of dish, then coconut, then chocolate chips, then peanut butter chips. Drizzle the sweetened condensed milk evenly over layers. Sprinkle the nuts over top. Bake for 25 to 30 minutes, until set. Cut into squares while still warm.

Blueberry Crisp

6 to 9 servings

This makes me think of garden time, but it makes no difference whether you use frozen or fresh berries 'cause everyone will think you just came from the berry patch. And when you serve it with a scoop of vanilla ice cream . . . "Crisp à La Mode."

4 cups blueberries, thawed if frozen

1 tablespoon lemon juice

1 cup sugar

2½ tablespoons cornstarch

½ teaspoon ground cinnamon

½ teaspoon ground nutmeg

½ teaspoon fresh grated lemon peel

TOPPING

½ box plain yellow cake mix

8 tablespoons (1 stick) butter, melted

½ cup chopped pecans

Preheat oven to 350°F. Put the blueberries in a medium-sized bowl, add the lemon juice, and toss gently. Mix together the sugar, cornstarch, cinnamon, nutmeg, and lemon peel. Add the blueberries and mix gently. Turn into a greased 9-inch square baking pan or casserole dish. Sprinkle the dry cake mix over top; drizzle with the melted butter and sprinkle with the pecans. Bake for 45 to 50 minutes, or until golden brown. Serve warm or cold with ice cream.

NOTE: A full box of cake mix is 18.25 ounces. Use half now and save the other half for next time—which should be very soon!

Italian Christmas Cream

8 to 10 servings

This one's holiday-colorful, smooth, and fresh. It's just what you need during the busy holiday season 'cause it's simple and special all in one! It's just mixing and freezing, but it tastes like a creamy Italian homemade specialty. And does it ever look great on a table with all those colors!

- 2 medium-sized firm bananas, peeled and sliced
- 1 cup sliced seedless green grapes
- 2 cups (16 ounces) sour cream
- 1 cup coarsely chopped Maraschino cherries
- 1 cup coarsely chopped walnuts
- ½ cup sugar
- 1½ teaspoons grated fresh lemon peel

Combine all ingredients in a large bowl; mix well. Pour into a 2-quart shallow casserole dish or mold lightly coated with a nonstick vegetable spray. Freeze overnight. Let stand at room temperature for 15 to 20 minutes before serving; you can unmold it onto a serving plate if desired.

rozen Pumpkin Pie

6 to 8 servings

Holiday times can be so hectic. Wouldn't it be nice to make dessert ahead of time and still get raves? Well, this one will do it, because it's holiday special without the holiday rush.

1 cup canned pumpkin

⅔ cup light corn syrup

½ teaspoon ground cinnamon

¼ teaspoon ground nutmeg

¼ teaspoon ground ginger

½ cup coarsely chopped walnuts

1 container (8 ounces) frozen whipped topping, thawed

1 prepared 9-inch graham cracker pie crust

Combine the pumpkin, corn syrup, spices, and nuts in a large bowl. Fold in the whipped topping. Spoon mixture into crust. Freeze until firm, about 4 hours. Let stand at room temperature for 15 minutes before serving.

NOTE: I like to top it with extra whipped topping before serving.

Blueberry Cream Pie

6 to 8 servings

Here's another no-bake pie with great summertime taste. You can enjoy the warm weather flavor any time of the year by substituting frozen or canned blueberries. Any way you slice it, they'll be asking for more.

1 can (14 ounces) sweetened condensed milk

Juice of 2 lemons

½ cup heavy cream

2 cups fresh blueberries (well dried after rinsing)

1 cup frozen whipped topping, thawed (an 8-ounce container is 3½ cups)

1 prepared 9-inch graham cracker pie crust

Frozen whipped topping, thawed, for garnish (optional)

Fresh blueberries for garnish (optional)

In a large bowl, stir together the sweetened condensed milk, lemon juice, and heavy cream. In another large bowl, gently combine the blueberries and whipped topping. Fold the blueberry mixture into the milk-cream mixture and mound it into the pie crust. Chill in the refrigerator for at least 6 to 8 hours or overnight. Garnish each serving with additional whipped topping and a few fresh blueberries, if desired.

NOTE: Use frozen unsugared blueberries or unsugared canned blueberries, drained well, if substituting for fresh berries.

Peach Crumble

If you bought too many peaches and they're starting to shrivel, don't worry! You can turn them into a perfect Peach Crumble. It'll taste terrific and there are other good things about it, too: It's an easy cleanup and it freezes well, so you can make extra and enjoy it for a long time afterward.

4 cups sliced fresh peaches	**¾ teaspoon ground nutmeg**
¾ cup firmly packed brown sugar	**5⅓ tablespoons (⅓ cup) butter, softened**

TOPPING

1 cup graham cracker crumbs

¾ teaspoon ground cinnamon

Preheat oven to 375°F. In a small bowl, mix together all the topping ingredients. Combine peaches and brown sugar in an 8-inch square baking pan. Sprinkle topping evenly over the peaches. Bake for 30 to 35 minutes, until peaches are soft and topping is bubbly.

NOTE: This is great served with ice cream.

Creamy Rice and Apple Pudding

6 servings

Everybody loves good old-fashioned rice pudding and now we can make it extra special by adding fresh apples for the best of all worlds! Fresh, smooth, creamy, and delicious!

2½ cups milk

¾ cup quick-cooking rice

¼ cup firmly packed light brown sugar

½ teaspoon salt

2 eggs, lightly beaten

½ cup coarsely chopped (peeled) apple (about 1 small apple)

1½ teaspoons vanilla extract

¼ cup coarsely chopped walnuts

In a medium-sized saucepan, combine the milk, rice, sugar, and salt; bring to a boil. Reduce heat and simmer, uncovered, for 5 minutes, stirring occasionally. Beat 2 tablespoons of the hot rice mixture into the eggs, beating constantly; stir this mixture into the rice mixture remaining in saucepan. Stir in the chopped apple. Cook and stir over low heat for 30 seconds longer; *do not boil.* Remove from heat, stir in the vanilla extract, and pour into a large serving bowl or individual serving dishes. Cover and refrigerate until thoroughly chilled. Sprinkle with the chopped nuts before serving.

NOTE: I like to use golden delicious apples because they don't turn brown as fast as other apples. The pudding thickens when chilled.

elf-Filled Cupcakes

30 cupcakes

Wanna raise some eyebrows? These are like having a cheesecake-filled chocolate cake. Think these will be appreciated? You bet! Did you ever wonder how they get that creamy filling inside those cupcakes at the bakery? Wait 'til you see how these turn out and you'll know the secret.

- 1 package (18.25 ounces) chocolate cake mix
- 1 package (8 ounces) cream cheese, softened
- ⅓ cup sugar
- 1 egg
- 6 ounces chocolate chips

Preheat oven to 350°F. Line muffin pans with paper baking cups. Make cake mix according to package directions. Spoon batter into muffin pans, filling each cup about two-thirds full. In a large bowl, beat the cream cheese and the sugar until light and fluffy. Beat in the egg. Stir in the chips. Drop 1 teaspoon of cheese mixture onto each cupcake. Bake as cake mix package directs.

ream Cheese Tarts

36 tarts

These are easy to make, easy to serve. They make great snack treats, party treats, anytime treats.

4 packages (8 ounces each) cream cheese, softened

1¼ cups sugar

4 eggs

2 teaspoons vanilla extract

1 can (21 ounces) cherry pie filling (or your favorite pie filling)

36 vanilla wafers

Preheat oven to 375°F. Line muffin pans with paper baking cups. In a large bowl, beat together the cream cheese, sugar, eggs, and vanilla extract. Place a vanilla wafer in the bottom of each muffin cup. Spoon cream cheese mixture over vanilla wafer, filling each cup about two-thirds full. Top each with 1 teaspoon pie filling. Bake for 15 to 20 minutes. Let cool, then refrigerate for several hours or until thoroughly chilled.

NOTE: These tarts come out of the oven a little soft but they'll firm up when you chill them.

Last-Minute Applesauce Dessert

6 servings

Need a dessert in a hurry? Here's one that's super-quick and delicious!

2 cups applesauce

1 teaspoon ground cinnamon

Dash nutmeg

¼ cup firmly packed brown sugar

1 teaspoon lemon juice

6 ½-inch slices pound cake

Whipped cream or frozen whipped topping, thawed, for garnish

In a large bowl, combine the applesauce, cinnamon, nutmeg, brown sugar, and lemon juice. Toast pound cake slices until golden brown on both sides. Put on serving plates and top with applesauce mixture. Garnish with whipped cream or whipped topping.

Spice Bars

25 to 30 bars

Autumn gets me thinking about spice cakes and cookies like Momma and Grandma used to make. These combine that old-fashioned taste with the easiness of today. And wait 'til you smell them baking!

¼ cup vegetable oil

1 cup sugar

¼ cup honey

2 cups all-purpose flour

1½ teaspoons ground cinnamon

1 teaspoon baking soda

½ teaspoon salt

1 egg, well beaten

1 cup chopped pecans

GLAZE

1 cup confectioners' sugar

1 tablespoon water

1 teaspoon vanilla extract

2 tablespoons butter or margarine, melted

Preheat oven to 350°F. In a large bowl, mix the oil, sugar, and honey. Add the flour, cinnamon, baking soda, and salt; mix well. Add the egg and pecans; mix well. Press mixture into an ungreased 10"x15" baking pan. Bake for 20 minutes. Meanwhile, beat together all glaze ingredients until smooth. Drizzle glaze over the top of the warm spice bars, cut into squares, and serve warm.

Peanut Butter Cream Pie

6 to 8 servings

Peanut butter is an all-American favorite. Well, here's another way to enjoy it. It's a "just mix it up" that you can make ahead for weekend company, or keep in the refrigerator for after-school snacks.

- 4 tablespoons (¼ cup) butter
- 2 cups milk
- ⅓ cup sugar
- ½ teaspoon salt
- 4 tablespoons cornstarch
- ½ cup water
- 4 egg yolks
- 3 tablespoons creamy peanut butter

- 1 baked 9-inch pie shell
- Whipped cream for topping
- ¼ cup coarsely chopped peanuts or ¼ cup miniature chocolate chips (optional)

In a large saucepan, combine the butter, milk, sugar, and salt. Bring to a boil, stirring occasionally. Meanwhile, in a medium-sized bowl, whisk cornstarch and water until smooth, then whisk in the egg yolks. Whisk egg mixture into the boiling milk mixture and stir until thick, over medium heat. Remove from heat and stir in peanut butter. Pour into baked pie shell. Chill and then top with whipped cream. Top with nuts or miniature chocolate chips, if desired.

Death by Chocolate

feeds up to 24 (or 1 serious chocoholic!)

The name is so sinfully descriptive of the taste. If you want to be the hit of the family, the hit of the neighborhood, the hit of whatever, just serve Death by Chocolate. It's easy and convenient, 'cause you can make it in advance, and you'll have plenty of time to take your bows. Do you know anyone who could do anything but love even the thought of this?

- 1 box (19.8 ounces) fudge brownie mix

- ¼ to ½ cup coffee liqueur

- 3 packages (3.5 ounces each) instant chocolate mousse

- 8 chocolate-covered toffee candy bars (1.4 ounces each) (like Skor® or Heath® bars)

- 1 container (12 ounces) frozen whipped topping, thawed

Preheat oven according to brownie package directions. Bake brownies according to package directions; let cool. Prick holes in the tops of brownies with a fork and pour the coffee liqueur over brownies; set aside. Prepare chocolate mousse according to package directions. Break candy bars into small pieces in food processor or by gently tapping the wrapped bars with a hammer. Break up half the brownies into small pieces and place in the bottom of a large glass bowl or trifle dish. Cover with half the mousse, then half the candy, and then half the whipped topping. Repeat layers with the remaining ingredients.

NOTE: Instead of the coffee liqueur, you may substitute a mixture of 1 teaspoon sugar and 4 tablespoons leftover black coffee, or just leave out the coffee flavoring entirely.

Old-Fashioned Bread Pudding

6 servings

This is one of my favorite recipes for bread pudding 'cause it's easy and it tastes like the good old days. Want to make it a little different and fancy? How about adding chopped apples or cherries, even chopped canned peaches or pears? Serve it cold or hot with maple syrup—any way you like it.

- 4 tablespoons (¼ cup) butter, softened
- 2 cups milk
- 2 eggs
- ½ cup sugar
- ¼ teaspoon salt
- 1 teaspoon ground cinnamon
- 3 cups soft bread cubes (about 5 slices bread)
- ½ cup raisins

Preheat oven to 350°F. Put the butter in a small bowl. Scald the milk (heat it to just below boiling), and pour it over the butter; stir to mix well. Beat the eggs in a large bowl. Gradually stir in milk mixture; stir in the sugar, salt, and cinnamon. Put the bread cubes and raisins in a 1½-quart baking dish; pour in milk mixture. Stir gently to moisten bread evenly. Set baking dish in a larger pan; add hot water to pan to come about halfway up sides of baking dish. Bake for 40 to 45 minutes or until knife inserted into pudding comes out clean. Serve warm or cold.

NOTE: Maple syrup, the *real* maple syrup that I grew up with—there's nothing like it. It's expensive, but a small bottle for topping French toast, pancakes, waffles, or a bread pudding like this one on a special day . . . it's well worth it. It's a natural taste that can't be duplicated.

Cookies in a Crust

6 to 8 servings

When I need a lift, I whip up a chocolate chip cookie pie, and you can, too. In fact, it's so easy that the kids can help make it before they help eat it. And don't be afraid to experiment. Feel like using chocolate chunks, more nuts, or no nuts at all? Go for it!

2 eggs

⅓ cup granulated sugar

⅓ cup all-purpose flour

⅓ cup firmly packed brown sugar

8 tablespoons (1 stick) butter or margarine, melted and cooled to room temperature

6 ounces chocolate chips

⅔ cup chopped walnuts

1 prepared 9-inch butter-flavored pie crust

Preheat oven to 325°F. In a large bowl, beat the eggs until foamy. Add the sugar, flour, and brown sugar and mix well. Stir in the melted butter; add the chocolate chips and walnuts. Pour into pie crust and bake for 50 minutes to 1 hour, until golden.

Frozen Pineapple-Lemon Pie

6 to 8 servings

Don't feel like heating up the kitchen but wanna put a great-tasting dessert on the table for your family? Well, everybody will have room for this one 'cause it's light and refreshing. And it keeps well in the freezer, so you can whip it up when you have the time. It's just the right top-off for a patio barbecue.

1 can (20 ounces) crushed pineapple in heavy syrup, drained (reserve 1 tablespoon syrup)

1 container (8 ounces) frozen whipped topping, thawed

½ cup chopped walnuts

Grated peel of 1 lemon

2 teaspoons lemon juice

1 prepared 9-inch graham cracker pie crust

In a large bowl, combine the pineapple, whipped topping, nuts, lemon peel, lemon juice, and 1 tablespoon reserved pineapple syrup. Stir until well blended and spoon into crust. Cover and freeze for several hours until firm, or overnight. Let stand at room temperature for 10 minutes before serving.

Raisin Cheesecake Pie

6 to 8 servings

What a perfect combo! This pie has that special holiday taste and look, but you can enjoy it any time. Just a hint: For a really fresh taste I like to spread on the topping just before serving.

1 cup (8 ounces) sour cream

½ cup sugar

2 eggs

1 tablespoon all-purpose flour

1 teaspoon ground cinnamon

¼ teaspoon ground allspice

¼ teaspoon salt

1 cup raisins

1 unbaked 9-inch pie shell

TOPPING

3 ounces cream cheese, softened

¾ cup sifted confectioners' sugar

1 cup heavy cream, whipped

Preheat oven to 350°F. In a large bowl, beat together the sour cream, sugar, eggs, flour, spices, and salt. Stir in the raisins and pour mixture into pie shell. Bake for 50 to 60 minutes or until toothpick inserted into center comes out clean. Let cool completely. To make topping, cream the cream cheese and confectioners' sugar. Fold in the whipped cream. Spread evenly over top of pie. Serve immediately or chill before serving.

NOTE: It's fine to use a store-bought pie shell.

Candy Bar Angel

6 to 9 servings

This is one of my favorites. It's a cool and creamy pudding-pleaser of a dessert. And if you wanna make a banana cream version, go ahead!

3 chocolate-covered toffee candy bars (1.4 ounces each) (like Skor® or Heath® bars)

1 packaged angel food cake (12 ounces)

1 package (5 ounces) instant vanilla pudding

1 teaspoon vanilla extract

1 container (12 ounces) frozen whipped topping, thawed

Crush the candy bars in a food processor, or gently tap the wrapped bars with a hammer or some other heavy object. Shred or crumble the angel food cake into small pieces and put into a 9-inch square baking dish. Mix the pudding according to package directions, adding the vanilla extract. Spoon pudding over the shredded cake, spread the whipped topping over the pudding, and sprinkle the crushed candy bars over the top. Serve immediately or chill before serving.

NOTE: For a different taste, I often use banana pudding instead of vanilla and add a layer of sliced bananas over the pudding. And if you want to use 4 candy bars instead of 3, that's fine, too.

Blueberry Cheesecake in a Glass

10 servings

Hooray! No baking! Don't you just love blueberry season? I can't get enough of 'em and this is a great variation of one of my favorites: blueberries and cream. But you don't have to enjoy this only in blueberry season, because frozen berries work fine, too.

2 packages (8 ounces each) cream cheese, softened

⅓ cup sifted confectioners' sugar

1⅓ cups sour cream

⅔ cup heavy cream or 1½ cups frozen whipped topping, thawed

Vanilla wafers (optional)

7 cups blueberries (about 3½ pints)

1 tablespoon orange-flavored liqueur (optional)

In a large bowl, mix together the cream cheese, confectioners' sugar, and sour cream until smooth. Whip the heavy cream and fold it into the cream cheese mixture. Put a vanilla wafer in the bottom of each of ten glasses. Toss the blueberries in orange-flavored liqueur, if desired. Fill the glasses about two-thirds full with berries. Add 3 tablespoons of the cream cheese mixture to each glass and lightly shake it down so it oozes over the berries. Add another tablespoon of berries to each glass, another tablespoon of cream cheese mixture, and top with a few berries. Serve immediately or refrigerate for an hour or two.

NOTE: Use your favorite stemmed glasses for this simple but elegant dessert.

Peanut Butter and Jelly Pie

6 to 8 servings

Peanut butter and jelly is everybody's favorite. Well, this is a great novel way to serve it to the gang. And you can use any flavor preserves—whatever tickles your fancy! But whichever flavor you use, they'll say, "Pie? Peanut Butter and Jelly Pie? Wow! More! More!"

- 1 package (8 ounces) cream cheese, softened
- 1/3 cup peanut butter
- 1/2 cup confectioners' sugar
- 1 tablespoon milk
- 1 prepared 9-inch chocolate-flavored pie crust
- 1/2 cup strawberry preserves
- 2 cups frozen whipped topping, thawed (an 8-ounce container is 3 1/2 cups)

In a large bowl, combine the cream cheese and peanut butter, mixing until well blended. Add the sugar and milk; mix well. Spoon cream cheese mixture into pie crust; chill. Spread with the preserves; top with whipped topping.

Apple Chiffon Mousse

9 servings

You can use your own homemade applesauce or store-bought applesauce. Either way, you'll feel great serving this fancy-tasting, easy-making mousse. And if you want a little variety, whip up some Very Berry Sauce. I don't think the mousse has to have it, but for a simple gourmet-looking and gourmet-tasting dessert for that fancy dinner party, it'll work like a charm!

2 cups applesauce

3 egg whites

½ cup sugar

1 tablespoon lemon juice

1 teaspoon vanilla extract

1 cup heavy cream

VERY BERRY SAUCE

1 tablespoon cornstarch

1 tablespoon cold water

1 package (10 ounces) frozen strawberries, thawed and drained (reserve liquid)

1 package (10 ounces) frozen raspberries, thawed and drained (reserve liquid)

2 teaspoons orange-flavored liqueur (optional)

In a large bowl, combine the applesauce, egg whites, sugar, lemon juice, and vanilla. Beat with an electric mixer at high speed until light and fluffy. Whip the cream; fold it into applesauce mixture. Spoon the mousse into an 8- or 9-inch square pan. Freeze until firm or overnight. Meanwhile, to make Very Berry Sauce, mix cornstarch and cold water in a small bowl or cup; stir until smooth. In a small saucepan, combine the cornstarch mixture and the reserved fruit liquids. Cook over medium heat until mixture thickens and becomes clear. Remove from heat and let cool. Stir in the berries; stir in the liqueur, if desired. Refrigerate until chilled. Cut frozen mousse into 9 squares. Top each serving with some of the sauce.

NOTE: You can freeze the mousse in individual molds or custard cups, if you like; simply invert to serve.

Georgia Bread Pudding

8 to 9 servings

This is a great make-ahead dessert for home entertaining. At serving time you can relax—the pressure is off!

1 cup sugar

1 can (12 ounces) evaporated milk

2 cups whole milk

4 egg yolks

5⅓ tablespoons (⅓ cup) butter, melted

¼ cup raisins

1 teaspoon vanilla extract

⅛ teaspoon ground cinnamon

⅛ teaspoon ground nutmeg

9 slices white bread with crusts, cut into cubes

Preheat oven to 400°F. In a large bowl, thoroughly mix the sugar, evaporated and whole milk, and egg yolks. Add the melted butter, raisins, vanilla extract, and spices; mix well. Add the bread cubes and toss to saturate bread. Pour mixture into a greased 8-inch square baking dish. Bake for 25 minutes until pudding is lightly browned and set. Let cool before cutting. (The pudding will get firmer and be easier to cut when cool.) Cut into squares; reheat slightly in the microwave before serving, if desired.

Banana Breeze Pie

6 to 8 servings

Want to be the hit at all the parties? Then make this pie and listen to the rave reviews. Great served with whipped topping, too.

5⅓ tablespoons (⅓ cup) butter or margarine

¼ cup sugar

½ teaspoon ground cinnamon (optional)

1 cup corn flake crumbs

1 package (8 ounces) cream cheese, softened

1 can (14 ounces) sweetened condensed milk

⅓ cup plus 2 table-spoons lemon juice

1 teaspoon vanilla extract

5 medium-sized bananas

In a small pan, melt the butter over low heat; stir in the sugar and cinnamon and cook until bubbles form. Remove from heat. Stir in the crumbs. Press mixture evenly over the bottom and up the sides of a 9-inch pie pan; chill. Meanwhile, in a large bowl, beat the cream cheese until fluffy; blend in the sweetened condensed milk. Add the ⅓ cup lemon juice and the vanilla; stir until smooth and thick. Cut 3 of the bananas into thin slices, line bottom of chilled crust with banana slices. Turn filling into crust. Refrigerate for 2 to 3 hours or until firm. Cut remaining 2 bananas into thin slices; dip slices in remaining 2 tablespoons lemon juice. Arrange banana slices over top of pie.

NOTE: Be sure to use exactly ⅓ cup lemon juice in the filling.

Chocolate Chip Raisin Rewards

16 squares

Wrap these in plastic wrap and they'll travel anywhere with you. Great for picnics, car trips, lunch boxes, anytime.

- 1 cup all-purpose flour
- ½ teaspoon baking powder
- ¼ teaspoon baking soda
- ¼ teaspoon salt
- 8 tablespoons (1 stick) butter, softened
- ½ cup firmly packed brown sugar
- 1 egg
- 2 tablespoons milk
- 1 teaspoon vanilla extract
- ½ cup raisins
- ½ cup chocolate chips
- ½ cup chopped walnuts

Preheat oven to 350°F. In a medium-sized bowl, combine the flour, baking powder, baking soda, and salt. Cream the butter in a large bowl; gradually add the brown sugar and beat until smooth and well blended. Beat in the egg, milk, and vanilla. Gradually beat in the flour mixture. Stir in the raisins, chocolate chips, and nuts. Spread into a greased 8-inch square baking pan. Bake for 25 to 30 minutes. Cool on wire rack; cut into squares.

Key Lime Pie Cheesecake

6 to 8 servings

This is as simple as Key Lime Pie, but smoother and creamier. Feel those breezes, that warm sunshine? This may not be the same as a few days in the islands but it will sure make dessert time a tropical pleasure.

1 package (8 ounces) cream cheese, softened

1 can (14 ounces) sweetened condensed milk

1 container (12 ounces) frozen whipped topping, thawed

1 cup fresh lime juice (about 5 limes)

1 baked 9-inch pie shell

Lime slices and fresh mint leaves for garnish (optional)

In a large bowl, combine the cream cheese, sweetened condensed milk, and whipped topping. Stir in the lime juice until well blended and mixture is thick and smooth. Immediately pour lime filling into pie shell. Pie can be served at once, but for best flavor, chill it for about 2 hours. Garnish with fresh lime slices and fresh mint leaves, if desired.

NOTE: Another nice way to serve this is topped with whipped cream or whipped topping and sprinkled with grated lime rind—looks even fresher and more scrumptious.

Lemon Creamsicles™

12 frozen pops

Here's something the kids will gobble up! (That's if there are any left after the adults get through with them.) And for a different flavor, how about lime Creamsicles™? Makes a great summer fun snack but you can really enjoy them anytime.

1 can (14 ounces) sweetened condensed milk

½ teaspoon fresh grated lemon rind

½ cup fresh lemon juice

⅓ cup sugar

1 cup milk

12 Popsicle™ sticks

In a large bowl, combine all ingredients and stir until sugar dissolves. Pour mixture into 12 small (2- to 3-ounce) molds or paper cups and insert a Popsicle™ stick into the center of each. Freeze for 3 to 6 hours, or until solid.

Easy Peanut Butter Cookies

4 dozen

Last-minute company? Need something in a hurry? These are fast and delicious! However, you're probably gonna want these around all the time, company or not!

1 can (14 ounces) sweetened condensed milk

¾ cup peanut butter

2 cups biscuit baking mix

1 teaspoon vanilla extract

Sugar

Preheat oven to 375°F. In a large mixing bowl, beat the sweetened condensed milk and peanut butter until smooth. Beat in the biscuit mix and vanilla extract; mix well. Shape dough into 1-inch balls; roll in sugar. Place balls 2 inches apart on ungreased baking sheets. Flatten cookies with a fork. Bake for 6 to 8 minutes or until lightly browned (do not overbake). Cool in pan. Store, tightly covered, at room temperature.

NOTE: For a nice variation called Peanut Blossoms, do not flatten the balls of dough. Bake as above; remove from oven, and press a milk chocolate candy kiss into the center of each cookie.

Newer Ambrosia

8 servings

This is a wonderful throw-together dessert that will remind you of the fifties but has today's easy, great taste.

1½ cups miniature marshmallows

1 can (20 ounces) pineapple chunks in heavy syrup, drained

1 can (11 ounces) mandarin oranges, drained

1 cup shredded coconut

1 cup (8 ounces) sour cream

6 Maraschino cherries, cut in half (optional)

Crushed nuts for garnish (optional)

In a large bowl, combine all the ingredients and toss gently. Refrigerate for 2 to 3 hours to marry the flavors. (Overnight is even better!) Sprinkle on some crushed nuts, if you'd like.

Bread Box Pudding

4 to 6 servings

Hate to throw away those stale muffins or donuts, that old bread? Well, now you don't have to. Serve this hot or cold, with ice cream or whipped cream, and you'll turn guilt into glad.

2 cups cubed day-old bread	1 cup milk
2 cups coarsely crumbled leftover doughnuts, Danish, muffins, or cookies	⅓ cup honey
	1 tablespoon vanilla extract
	1 teaspoon ground cinnamon
5 eggs, beaten	¼ cup raisins

Preheat oven to 325°F. Combine all ingredients in a large bowl. Pour mixture into a greased 1½-quart baking dish. Bake for 35 to 40 minutes or until set. Serve warm or chilled, plain or with whipped topping or ice cream.

Filled Pineapple Pots

24 cupcakes

Kids of all ages will love these treats. I mean ALL ages! Even kids like me!

1 box (18.25 ounces) yellow cake mix

1 can (20 ounces) pineapple chunks in natural juice, drained (reserve juice)

Water

12 Maraschino cherries, halved

Confectioners' sugar (optional)

Preheat oven according to package directions. Line two 12-cup muffin pans with paper baking cups. Make the cake batter, using reserved pineapple juice plus water for the liquid called for on the cake box. Drop half a cherry and one chunk of pineapple into each cup. (If there are leftover chunks, halve them and drop them in, too.) Fill each cup about three-quarters full with batter. Bake according to package directions. When cooled, dust with confectioners' sugar if desired.

NOTE: For a different look and taste, you can add blueberries along with the pineapple chunks. You can also top these with your favorite icing.

Fresh Blender Applesauce

4 to 6 servings

Have some mushy apples you want to get rid of? They're fine for this (of course, fresh ones are great, too). So is any variety or size or combination of varieties. I like this applesauce chilled, but it's also just as good at room temperature. And it's a lot easier than cooking!

3 to 4 golden delicious apples, peeled, cored, and cut into chunks

¼ cup honey

¼ cup apple juice or cider

2 teaspoons lemon juice

Place all ingredients in the container of a food processor or an electric blender. Process just until smooth. Serve at room temperature or chilled.

Peanut Butter Chocolate Candy Cookies

25 to 30 bars

Do you like delicious? Well, who doesn't? These are sure to become a family favorite. Wait 'til you taste them—they taste like homemade peanut butter cups!

1 cup creamy peanut butter	1 cup graham cracker crumbs
½ pound (2 sticks) butter, melted	12 ounces chocolate chips, melted
1 pound confectioners' sugar	

In a large bowl, mix together the peanut butter, butter, confectioners' sugar, and graham cracker crumbs. Spread the mixture in a well-greased 10"x15" baking pan. Pour the melted chocolate chips evenly over mixture. Refrigerate for 15 minutes. Slice into bars, but leave in pan. Refrigerate until well chilled; serve cold.

Chocolate Chip Cheesecake

15 to 20 servings

This is so sinful but so delicious. You'll surely make this a standard. Wait 'til you taste it!

- 3 packages (8 ounces each) cream cheese, softened
- 3 eggs
- ¾ cup sugar
- 1 teaspoon vanilla extract
- 2 rolls (20 ounces each) refrigerator chocolate chip cookie dough

Preheat oven to 350°F. In a large bowl, beat together the cream cheese, eggs, sugar, and vanilla until well mixed; set aside. Slice cookie dough rolls into ⅓-inch slices. Arrange slices from one roll over the bottom of a greased 9"x13" baking dish; press together so there are no holes in dough. Spoon cream cheese mixture evenly over dough; top with remaining slices of cookie dough. Bake for 45 to 50 minutes, or until golden and center is slightly firm. Remove from oven, let cool, then refrigerate. Cut into slices when well chilled.

NOTE: You can serve the cheesecake plain, with chocolate sauce, with fudge or whipped topping—whatever is your favorite.

Pistachio Holiday

about 25 cookies

If you love pistachio nuts as much as I do, you'll love these. Are they ever light and yummy!

2 egg whites (at room temperature)

½ teaspoon vanilla extract

½ teaspoon ground cinnamon

½ cup sugar

1 cup (about 5 ounces) natural California pistachios, shelled and finely chopped (you should have ½ cup after chopping)

Preheat oven to 325°F. Line a cookie sheet with brown paper. In a large bowl, beat the egg whites, vanilla, and cinnamon with an electric mixer until soft peaks form. Gradually beat in the sugar; beat until stiff peaks form. Fold in the chopped pistachios. Drop by teaspoonfuls onto prepared cookie sheet. Bake for 20 minutes. Turn off oven and leave cookies in oven until cool.

NOTE: I like to use the smooth side of a brown paper shopping bag to line the cookie sheet.

ranberry Pudding

about 8 servings

Cranberries are not only for holiday dinners. They're great all year long. And when you save them like this for dessert—boy, talk about holiday-type attention!

1¼ cups fresh cran-
berries

⅓ cup firmly packed
brown sugar

⅓ cup chopped
pecans

1 egg, beaten

½ cup granulated
sugar

½ cup all-purpose
flour

5⅓ tablespoons
(⅓ cup) butter,
melted

Preheat oven to 325°F. Put the cranberries in a medium-sized bowl. Sprinkle the brown sugar over cranberries, and toss gently. Mix in the chopped pecans, and turn into an ungreased 9-inch pie plate. In another medium-sized bowl, combine all remaining ingredients and mix well. Pour over cranberry mixture. Bake for 45 minutes.

NOTE: Serve hot or cold with whipped cream or ice cream.

HODGEPODGE

Here's a batch of recipes that didn't quite fit into any particular section of the book but are some of the most requested from my TV show. Some save time or money or work, but all are delicious. Flip through them and you're bound to see something that'll help you—they help me.

Blackened Seasoning Blend

about ¼ cup

Sprinkling this mixture on fish, meats, or chicken toward the end of broiling or sautéeing will give you that great Cajun taste without all the smoke. Believe me, sprinkling makes a lot more sense and you'll still enjoy the goodness.

- 1 tablespoon paprika
- 2 teaspoons dried thyme, crushed
- 1 teaspoon onion powder
- 1 teaspoon garlic powder
- 1 teaspoon salt
- 1 teaspoon sugar
- ½ teaspoon cayenne pepper
- 1 teaspoon black pepper

In a small bowl, combine all the ingredients and mix well. Store in a tightly covered jar.

NOTE: This recipe can easily be doubled or tripled; make it hotter or milder to your taste by varying the amounts of the ingredients.

No-Salt Herb Blend

about 1 cup

There are so many great spices, herbs, and blends. Experiment with this one and enjoy all the wonderful flavors!

4 tablespoons dried oregano	4 teaspoons garlic powder
4 tablespoons onion powder	2 teaspoons dried thyme
4 teaspoons dried marjoram	2 teaspoons dried rosemary
4 teaspoons dried basil	1 teaspoon dried sage
4 teaspoons ground savory	1 teaspoon pepper

In a medium-sized bowl, combine all ingredients. Crush with the back of a spoon, or transfer small amounts to a mortar and pestle and crush. Store in a shaker or tightly covered container.

NOTE: Sprinkle over fish, chicken, salads, or vegetables.

Salad Seasoning Blend

about 1 cup

Wait 'til you taste this over greens, tomatoes, cold veggies, or cottage cheese. Combined with oil and vinegar, it also makes a great salad dressing!

- ⅓ cup sesame seed
- 4½ tablespoons onion powder
- 2 tablespoons poppy seed
- 1½ tablespoons garlic powder
- 1½ tablespoons paprika
- ¾ teaspoon celery seed
- ¼ teaspoon pepper

Toast sesame seeds in a heavy skillet, stirring them over medium heat until golden, 3 to 5 minutes. Mix all remaining ingredients in a small bowl, and stir in toasted sesame seeds. Store in a shaker or tightly covered container.

Seeded Salad Dressing

1 cup

- ¾ cup vegetable oil
- ¼ cup cider vinegar
- 2 teaspoons Salad Seasoning Blend

Mix all ingredients in a jar. Cover and shake well. Use immediately or store in the refrigerator.

Seafood Seasoning Blend

about 1 tablespoon

Start with this simple mix-together seasoning blend and people will marvel at all the wonderful things you can do with seafood. It's one of the miracle blends to have on the shelf that can give a fresh special touch to whatever seafood we choose.

1 teaspoon dried dillweed	½ teaspoon onion salt
½ teaspoon dried basil	¼ teaspoon white pepper

Mix all ingredients together in a small bowl. Store in a tightly covered container. Use as is or as the base for Seafood Sauce, Dip, or Sauté.

Seafood Sauce

about 1⅔ cups

1 recipe Seafood Seasoning Blend	3 tablespoons white wine
1⅓ cups sour cream	1 tablespoon lemon or lime juice
¼ cup mayonnaise	

In a medium-sized bowl, combine all ingredients and mix thoroughly. Chill for at least 2 hours to blend flavors.

NOTE: Serve with steamed shrimp or crab, or baked or steamed fish.

Seafood Dip

about 1 quart

1 recipe Seafood Seasoning Blend (page 256)

2 packages (8 ounces each) cream cheese, softened

1 can (10¾ ounces) condensed cream of shrimp soup

1 pound cooked shrimp, peeled, deveined, and chopped, or 4 cans (4¼ ounces each) broken shrimp, drained

In a large bowl, beat together the Seafood Seasoning Blend, cream cheese, and soup until smooth. Fold in the shrimp. Chill for at least 2 hours to blend flavors

NOTE: You can substitute other cooked seafood for the shrimp if desired. Serve with crackers or cut-up veggies.

Seafood Sauté (Basting Butter)

about ½ cup

1 recipe Seafood Seasoning Blend (page 256)

8 tablespoons (1 stick) butter or margarine, softened

2 tablespoons lemon or lime juice

In a small bowl, whisk together all ingredients.

NOTE: Use when sautéeing seafood (this is enough for about 1 pound of seafood). This may also be used to baste seafood when grilling or broiling.

Creamy Pepper Dressing

about 3 cups

This is my favorite salad dressing, and it's also a great base for other dressings. Just add other seasonings like minced garlic for garlic dressing or chopped fresh dill for dill dressing. You get the picture!

- 2 cups mayonnaise
- ½ cup milk
- ¼ cup water
- 2 tablespoons freshly grated Parmesan cheese
- 1 tablespoon freshly ground black pepper
- 1 tablespoon cider vinegar
- 1 teaspoon fresh lemon juice
- 1 teaspoon finely chopped onion
- 1 teaspoon garlic salt
- Dash hot pepper sauce
- Dash Worcestershire sauce

In a large bowl, mix all ingredients until well blended. Chill well before using.

Blender Caesar Salad Dressing

4 to 6 servings

You don't have to go to a restaurant to get a great Caesar salad. Keep adding and subtracting ingredients in this one until you get it just the way you like it.

2 heads romaine lettuce

1 to 2 garlic cloves

⅔ cup olive oil

2 tablespoons wine vinegar (red or white)

Juice of 1 lemon

2 2-minute boiled eggs or 2 raw egg yolks

1 can (2 ounces) anchovy fillets

1½ to 2 tablespoons grated Parmesan cheese

¼ teaspoon pepper

4 tablespoons croutons (optional)

In a blender jar, blend the garlic, olive oil, vinegar, lemon juice, eggs, and anchovy fillets until well mixed. Put dressing in a large salad bowl. In cold water, rinse clean the romaine lettuce; dry well, and tear into bite-sized pieces. Add lettuce to salad bowl. Sprinkle with the Parmesan cheese, black pepper, and croutons, if desired. Toss well.

NOTE: Be sure to store in the refrigerator until ready to use. Refrigerate leftovers.

Summer Noodles

3 to 4 servings

Here's a light and fast dish for when you don't feel like fussing. And there are no rules! Wanna add your favorite seasoning? Do it! Have some leftover vegetables? Throw 'em in! It's easy and delicious, and you can make it a little different each time.

1 pound egg noodles (wide, medium, or fine)

1 cup (8 ounces) sour cream

1 pound cottage cheese

Salt and pepper to taste

In a large pot of boiling water, cook the noodles until just tender. Drain and put into a large bowl. Add the sour cream, cottage cheese, salt, and pepper, and toss lightly to coat.

NOTE: You can add chopped parsley and scallions, some Parmesan cheese, a dash of garlic powder, and/or dill or caraway seed and bake this at 325°F. for 15 to 20 minutes to make it into a casserole. Or add lightly cooked broccoli, green beans, zucchini, or any other in-season vegetable. Do your own thing!

heese Strata

4 to 6 servings

I like to create different flavors by adding "extras" like chopped peppers, sliced mushrooms, canned fried onions, or crumbled bacon. Then it's like having something a little bit different every time, but with the same E-A-S-Y.

8 slices white bread, crusts removed	1 teaspoon dry mustard
1 cup (4 ounces) shredded sharp Cheddar cheese	¼ teaspoon onion powder
1 cup (4 ounces) shredded Swiss cheese	Pinch cayenne pepper (optional)
3 eggs	¼ teaspoon salt
1½ cups milk	¼ teaspoon pepper

Preheat oven to 325°F. Lightly toast the bread. Place 4 slices in the bottom of a buttered 8-inch square baking dish. Sprinkle half the Cheddar and half the Swiss cheeses evenly over the bread. Lay the remaining 4 slices of bread over cheese; top with remaining shredded cheeses. In a large bowl, beat the eggs and milk together until well mixed; add the seasonings and beat just to mix. Pour mixture over the bread and cheese. Let sit for 15 to 20 minutes, then bake for 30 to 35 minutes, or until set.

NOTE: After baking for 30 minutes, you may want to remove strata from oven, top with your favorite "extra," and bake for an additional 10 minutes.

Tropical Summer Punch

4½ quarts

This is festive and easy to throw together for all kinds of summer fun—or for any time you want to feel like summer. Great for last-minute guests, graduations, backyard parties . . . whatever.

1 can (20 ounces) pineapple chunks in natural juice

1 can (12 ounces) frozen orange juice concentrate, thawed

1 can (6 ounces) frozen limeade concentrate, thawed

1 quart ginger ale, chilled

1 quart cranberry juice, chilled

2 cups (16 ounces) apple juice, chilled

1 package (10 ounces) frozen strawberries

1 lemon, thinly sliced

Combine the pineapple chunks (undrained) and orange juice and limeade concentrates in a punch bowl. Add 2 orange juice cans of water. Pour in the ginger ale, cranberry juice, and apple juice. Float frozen strawberries and lemon slices on top.

The Right Punch

3 quarts, about 25 servings

This one's bound to be popular at all your parties. And you can keep it cold by floating a pint of ice cream in it. Add a garnish of mint leaves for the breeze of a tropical paradise or sprinkle with nutmeg for the crispness of a winter wonderland. I told ya—all your parties.

- ½ gallon vanilla ice cream, softened
- 3 cups (24 ounces) pineapple juice, chilled
- ⅔ cup orange juice
- 1 tablespoon lemon juice
- 1 quart cold milk

Combine all ingredients in a large bowl and beat until frothy. Pour into a chilled punch bowl.

NOTE: Ice cream should be very soft.

Cream Cheese Frosting

about 2½ cups (enough for a 9"x13" sheet cake)

Great for any type of cake—especially carrot, spice, and pumpkin, because they become more special with this delicious frosting and your own special touches—a sprinkling of nuts, a dash or two of food coloring, whatever you like. It'll taste like you fussed, but you'll know the truth.

- 1 package (8 ounces) cream cheese, softened
- 8 tablespoons (1 stick) butter, softened
- 1 box (16 ounces) confectioners' sugar
- 1 tablespoon vanilla extract
- ½ to 1 cup chopped walnuts (optional)

In a large mixing bowl, beat the cream cheese and butter until smooth and creamy. Gradually beat in the sugar until well blended. Beat in the vanilla. Stir in chopped walnuts, if desired.

Creamy Fruit Dressing

about 2 cups

You can spoon this over any fruit for sweet, mellow, and delicious results. If you like, put a dollop of whipped cream over it and call it Fresh Fruit Chantilly. It only looks, sounds, and tastes fancy!

1 cup mayonnaise	4 tablespoons confectioners' sugar
1 cup (8 ounces) sour cream	
6 tablespoons frozen pineapple juice concentrate, thawed	4 tablespoons grated orange peel (fresh or dried)
	Dash allspice

In a bowl, mix all ingredients together well. Serve over cut-up fresh fruit.

Peach and Plum Jam

6 small jars

This jam freezes well. The only problem is, it usually disappears so fast that it never makes it to the freezer! It's homemade-delicious without the fuss. Everybody will be impressed because you made your own preserves!

4 cans (16 ounces each) peaches in light or heavy syrup, drained (about 6 cups)

3 cans (16½ ounces each) pitted canned plums, drained (about 4 cups)

2 cups sugar

2 tablespoons lemon juice

Preheat oven to 400°F. In a large bowl, mash the peaches and plums. Add the sugar and lemon juice; stir well. Pour into a 9"x13" glass baking dish. Bake, removing from oven and stirring frequently, until mixture almost reaches the consistency of jam (about 1 hour). When it cools, pour into jars or plastic containers and *refrigerate* or *freeze*.

NOTE: When the jam cools, it will thicken even more.

Pecans Bertolli

6 cups

Here's a great snack that will keep in the refrigerator for weeks or the freezer for months. You'll always be ready for entertaining. And here's a thought: they'd make a really nice house gift in a pretty tin or jar—just add ribbons!

6 cups pecan halves
(1 4-ounce can
is 1 cup)

1½ cups sugar

½ cup orange juice

½ cup water

¼ cup olive oil

½ teaspoon ground
cinnamon

Combine all ingredients in a large skillet. Cook over medium heat, stirring often, until liquid disappears and nuts have a glazed appearance. Pour onto a greased sheet pan. Using 2 forks, quickly separate and spread out nuts. Let cool completely. Store in a tightly covered container in the refrigerator or freezer.

Apple Crisp

8 servings

Couldn't resist that basket of beautiful apples? Well, here's an idea for using the extras. It's good hot or cold: plain, with ice cream, as a side dish for ham, poultry, or pork chops, or any way you like it. My favorite way? With ice cream, naturally, although whipped cream is up there in the voting, too!

- 1 package (8 ounces) corn bread stuffing
- 8 tablespoons (1 stick) butter or margarine, melted
- Grated rind of 1 orange
- 1 cup coarsely chopped nuts (pecans or walnuts)
- ½ teaspoon ground cinnamon
- ½ teaspoon ground mace (or nutmeg)
- 1 cup sugar
- 4½ pounds Granny Smith or other cooking apples, peeled, cored, and thickly sliced
- ½ cup water

Preheat oven to 350°F. In a large bowl, mix the stuffing, butter, orange rind, nuts, spices, and ⅓ cup of the sugar. Set aside. In another large bowl, mix the sliced apples, remaining ⅔ cup sugar, and water. Pour apple mixture into a greased 9″ x13″ baking pan. Spread crumb mixture evenly over apples. Bake for 40 to 45 minutes or until apples are easily pierced and juices are bubbly. Serve warm or cold.

Index

C

cabbage:
  creamy coleslaw, 174
  sunny slaw, 173
Caesar salad dressing,
    blender, 259
cake frostings:
  cream cheese, 264
  silky, 204–205
cakes:
  apple, "no bother," 213
  fabulous carrot, 204–205
  French coffee, 206–207
  self-filled cupcakes, 221
California chili chicken, 75
California fig–oat bran muf-
    fins, 188–189
California pistachio-stuffed
    mushrooms, 11
candy bar(s):
  angel, 231
  death by chocolate, 226
candy cookies, peanut butter
    chocolate, 246
caramel-glazed sweet pota-
    toes, 143
carrot(s):
  cake, fabulous, 204–205
  marinated, 177
catfish, onion-baked, 116
cauliflower pancakes, 170
Cheddar cheese:
  baked party dip, 6–7
  chicken pie, 56
  easy cheesy broccoli bake,
    179
  macaroni holiday, 159
  Mexican buffet, 12
  potato casserole, 135
  sausage 'n' egg casserole,
    105
  scalloped potatoes, 133
  smoky barbecue bean bake,
    169

special macaroni and, 158
stacked enchilada, 16
strata, 261
turkey buffet, 57
cheese:
  baked party dip, 6–7
  chicken pecan skillet, 71
  chicken pie, 56
  chili butter, 197
  corn mini-muffins, 196
  easy cheesy broccoli bake,
    179
  enchilada, stacked, 16
  fancy fast chicken, 60
  lasagna roll-ups, 156
  macaroni holiday, 159
  Mexican buffet, 12
  Mexican seasoned chicken
    croissants with, 79
  mini-pizza squares, 15
  nacho chips, California chili
    chicken with, 75
  the other baked potatoes,
    136
  Parmesan potato sticks, 134
  pasta and spinach, 151
  potato casserole, 135
  potato pudding, 137
  queso fundido, 13
  really rich rice, 145
  sauce, easy, 29
  sausage 'n' egg casserole,
    105
  scalloped potatoes, 133
  smoky barbecue bean bake,
    169
  special macaroni and, 158
  stacked enchilada, 16
  strata, 261
  summer noodles, 260
  turkey buffet, 81
  turkey lasagna, 154–155
  turkey twist salad, 161
  vegetable chowder, 45
  see also cream cheese

frikadeller (Danish meat-
    balls), 18
frostings:
  cream cheese, 264
  silky, 204–205
frozen pineapple-lemon pie,
    229
frozen pumpkin pie, 217
fruit:
  dip, 8
  dressing, creamy, 265
  *see also specific types of
    fruit*

G

garden rice salad, 148
garlic:
  green salad, 175
  peeling of, 4
  pepper sauce, 33
  shrimp, 115
garlicky chicken wings, 4
gazpacho, 43
gazpacho blanco (white gaz-
    pacho), 44
Georgia bread pudding, 236
glazed chicken wings, 3
glazed meatballs, 14
golden fish fillets, 129
gorgeous grasshopper pie,
    210–211
goulash stew, 98
graham cracker pie crust:
  blueberry cream pie, 218
  frozen pineapple-lemon pie,
    229
  frozen pumpkin pie, 217
  millionaire's pie, 211
  two-tone cheese pie, 209
graham crackers:
  peach crumble, 219
  peanut butter chocolate
    candy cookies, 246

praline squares, 207
  seven-layer cookies, 214
grasshopper pie, gorgeous,
    210–211
Greek cucumber salad, 178
green bean(s):
  pancakes, 170
  summer noodles, 260
grilled meat loaf, 92
grouper fillets, lemon, 126

H

haddock:
  fish and rice chowder, 46
  fisherman's stew, 39
  lemon fillets, 126
  one-pot French chowder, 37
  onion-baked, 116
  southern-style fish chili, 130
half-baked sweet potatoes
    with lemon butter
    sauce, 142
halibut:
  garlic, 115
  orange-broiled, 119
  teriyaki marinade for, 27
  wealthy-style, 124–125
ham:
  better baked beans, 167
  macaroni holiday, 159
  smoky barbecue bean bake,
    169
  souper stew, 38
herb blend, no-salt, 254
herbed:
  chicken, 68
  onion bread, easy, 190
herbs, "flavorprints" and,
    xiii–xiv
hodgepodge, 251–268
  apple crisp, 268
  blackened seasoning blend,
    253

blender Caesar salad dressing, 259
cheese strata, 261
cream cheese frosting, 264
creamy fruit dressing, 265
creamy pepper dressing, 258
no-salt herb blend, 254
peach and plum jam, 266
pecans Bertolli, 267
the right punch, 263
salad seasoning blend, 255
seafood seasoning blend, sauce, dip, and sauté, 256–257
seeded salad dressing, 255
summer noodles, 260
tropical summer punch, 262
honey:
   butter sauce, oven-fried chicken with, 69
   pecan pork cutlets, 107
   wine sauce, chicken breast with, 55
hot artichoke spread, 10
house shrimp dip, 7

I

ice cream:
   cone pie, 208
   cranberry pudding with, 249
   peach crumble with, 219
   the right punch, 263
imitation crabmeat:
   garlic, 115
   seafood salad, 127
   smart crabcakes, 121
island turkey supper, 73
Italian Christmas cream, 216

J

jam, peach and plum, 266
Jarlsberg cheese:
   chili butter, 197
   corn mini-muffins, 196
jelly and peanut butter pie, 233

K

key lime pie cheesecake, 239
kidney bean(s):
   California chili chicken, 75
   chili, 183
   easy chili, 96
   souper stew, 38
   southern-style fish chili, 130

L

lamb:
   chops, baked, 109
   roasting of, timetable for, 90
   stuffed peppers, spiced, 110–111
lasagna:
   roll-ups, 156
   turkey, 154–155
last-minute applesauce dessert, 223
lemon:
   butter sauce, half-baked sweet potatoes with, 142
   coconut chicken, eye-opener, 65
   creamsicles, 240
   fillets, 126
   grilled chicken, 64
   pineapple pie, frozen, 229

ABOUT THE AUTHOR

Art Ginsburg has been appearing as MR. FOOD® for over ten years and his show is now the largest food news insert segment in the nation, seen in over 150 cities.